Curriculum Adaptations
for Students with Learning
and Behavior Problems

Fall,
97

G.W.U.

Curriculum Adaptations for Students with Learning and Behavior Problems

Principles and Practices

· ·

SECOND EDITION

John J. Hoover
James R. Patton

pro·ed

8700 Shoal Creek Boulevard
Austin, Texas 78757-6897

pro·ed

©1997 by PRO-ED, Inc.
8700 Shoal Creek Boulevard
Austin, Texas 78757-6897

Publisher's Note: This book is an updated and expanded edition of *Curriculum Adaptation for Students with Learning and Behavior Problems: Principles and Practices* (Hoover, 1988) previously published through Hamilton Publications.

Library of Congress Cataloging-in-Publication Data

Hoover, John J.
    Curriculum adaptations for students with learning and behavior
  problems : principles and practices / John J. Hoover, James R.
  Patton. — 2nd ed.
        p.   cm.
    Includes bibliographical references and index.
    ISBN 0-89079-686-6 (pbk. : alk. paper)
    1. Learning disabled children—Education—United States–
  –Curricula.   2. Problem children—Education—United States–
  –Curricula.   3. Curriculum change—United States.   4. Curriculum
  planning—United States.   I. Patton, James R.   II. Title.
LC4705.H66   1997
371.926—dc20   96-36175
                                                              CIP

This book is designed in Goudy Regular and Italia.

Production Manager: Alan Grimes
Production Coordinator: Karen Swain
Managing Editor: Tracy Sergo
Art Director: Thomas Barkley
Reprints Buyer: Alicia Woods
Editor: Lisa Tippett
Editorial Assistant: Claudette Landry
Editorial Assistant: Suzi Hunn

Printed in the United States of America

2   3   4   5   6   7   8   9   10   01   00   99   98   97

Contents

. . . .

Preface

. . . .

As we move into the 21st century, educators are continuously reminded of the recurring challenges confronting students who have learning and behavior problems. Although progress has been made in the education of these students, building upon those efforts is critical if our schools are to move toward achieving effective education for all students, whether in special or inclusive settings. One of the most important and fundamental areas within education is the curriculum to which students are subjected and taught. Since the beginning of formal education in our K–12 system, educators have discussed, modified, tested, revised, and changed curricula. Although many of these efforts have created effective change, there are still many students who simply do not learn within prescribed curricula. These students require continuous modifications or adaptations in order to succeed in today's classroom, school, and home environments.

This second edition of *Curriculum Adaptation for Students with Learning and Behavior Problems: Principles and Practices* is about meeting the needs of students with less severe learning and behavior problems through ongoing and appropriate curriculum adaptations and modifications. The ideas, strategies, and procedures found within this book are appropriate for elementary and secondary students educated in special and inclusive education classrooms. Teachers of students in these grades will find numerous suggestions that challenge their students and also help create a classroom learning environment in which required school and district curricula in any subject area can be effectively adapted and implemented. This highly practical book provides the reader with an in-depth discussion of important issues related to the selection and implementation of curricular adaptations. The authors emphasize the notion that effective curriculum implementation and associated adaptations for students with learning and behavior problems best occur when educators possess an understanding of the total curriculum implementation process at the classroom level.

This book consists of five interrelated chapters. Chapter 1 provides an overview of current issues affecting a curriculum and its implementation, including the influences of the inclusive education movement on K–12 education. This chapter also offers varying viewpoints regarding definitions of curriculum; the particular definition used directly affects a teacher's approaches to implementing and adapting a curriculum. The four interrelated curricular elements—Content, Instructional Settings, Instructional Strategies, and Student Behaviors—are discussed in detail, along with the need to understand how these four elements affect each other as a curriculum is implemented on a daily basis. It is this interrelationship that creates the framework for successfully implementing and adapting the curriculum for students with learning and behavioral problems.

Chapters 2 and 3 focus on practical and effective strategies for adapting curricula for students with learning and behavior problems. Chapter 2 provides easy-to-use guides and checklists for identifying and implementing classroom curriculum adaptation needs for individual students. A process for adapting a curriculum is presented, along with discussions of learning style preferences and their relationships to effective implementation and adaptation. Chapter 3 gives numerous adaptation strategies, including strategies for adapting content, instructional settings, and instructional strategies and for modifying student behaviors. Teaching, learning, and study strategies are all discussed and presented in a format that facilitates easy application to the classroom. Chapter 3 also discusses the importance of cooperative learning in curriculum adaptation as well as use of current technologies. In Chapters 4 and 5 the authors explore the topics of program collaboration between special and inclusive educators and important student, parent, and educator concerns that must be considered in order to successfully adapt a curriculum for students with special learning needs. All of the chapters include several discussion issues to further the reader's understanding of the topics covered in the particular chapter.

This book is written primarily for practicing teachers and other educators who are responsible for the education of students with less severe learning and behavior problems. However, persons studying to be teachers will also find the contents of this book to be an asset as they pursue their teaching careers. It is our hope that special and inclusive education classroom teachers, as well as other persons concerned with the education of students with learning and behavior problems, will find this book to be a valuable resource.

Fundamentals of Curricula and Curriculum Adaptation

1

In recent years, various events have occurred that directly or indirectly affect the education of students with special learning needs. The influences of parental pressure, local administrative mandates, and state and federal legislation have all had an impact on curricula and their implementation. One result has been the requirement that, to the greatest extent possible, *all* students must follow some form of prescribed and mandated curriculum. This includes students with special learning needs. The requirement places increasing demands upon educators in their daily teaching activities to ensure that all students benefit from learning experiences associated with the mandated curricula. Educators who find themselves in a position where they must make adaptations to a curriculum thus must draw upon a knowledge base that encompasses several important issues related to curricula and adaptation.

This section considers several key curricular topics, including the educational issues of curricular definitions, types, elements, and conceptions and their associated implications (see Figure 1.1). Each major curricular issue is discussed briefly to provide the reader with a knowledge base upon which to make effective curriculum adaptation decisions. The term *curriculum adaptation*, as used throughout this book, refers to modifying or supplementing one or more curricular elements in order to meet the needs of individual students. This book emphasizes the concept that decisions related to curricular modifications or supplements are most effective when they are grounded in the concepts and issues discussed in this chapter, which provides an overview of educational issues regarding curricula, their impact on the academic placements of special education students, and subsequent effects upon implementation.

1

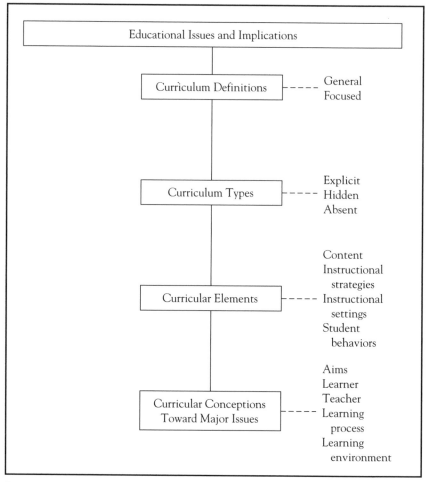

Figure 1.1.   Issues in curricula and curriculum implementation.

Educational Issues and Implications for Curricula

There are approximately 15,000 school districts in the United States, each of which has experienced various forms of social pressure as a result of political, ethical, and economic forces. In an increasing number of states, this social pressure has resulted in different legal mandates that dictate various aspects associated with curricula, including development, implementation, adaptation, and evaluation. A curriculum implemented in any one classroom reflects several levels of influence and associated decision making.

Table 1.1

Levels of Influence Affecting Curriculum Implementation

Level	Influences
National	Federal guidelines, legislation, and funding
State	Legislative mandates and funding, graduation requirements, time allotment for study of subjects
District	Allocations of resources and personnel
School	Specific distribution of resources and support assistance
Classroom	Teacher decision making concerning methods and use of materials

As teachers implement or adapt curricula at the classroom level, they are, in effect, implementing or adapting the product of numerous decisions made at different levels of the educational and political systems. These five different levels at which decisions directly or indirectly affect curricular implementation on a daily basis are illustrated in Table 1.1. The table also provides examples of various influences that may occur at each level. The first level is the national level, which reflects broader and more general influences; the last is the classroom level, where highly specific teacher influences prevail. In between these points are other levels that exert unique and important influences upon curricular implementation. The predominant theme illustrated by the five levels is that the curricular influences and issues relative to implementation and adaptations become more specific as one moves closer to the classroom level. The primary concern of most educators responsible for implementing curricula is what occurs at the classroom level. However, knowledge about the particular influences at each level provides these educators (who are actually implementing a curriculum) with additional insight into the development process and an explanation or rationale for the curriculum being implemented.

Inclusive Education

Currently, the most pervasive trend associated with the education of students with special needs involves the placement of these students in inclusive educational settings. The primary goal of the inclusion movement is to create a classroom environment where all students learn and have opportunities to work together (Stainback, Stainback, East, & Sapon-Sevin, 1995). This particular trend was preceded by other theories concerning the best educational placement for students with special needs. The predominant trends—likely special education placement(s), prevailing perspectives toward special education, and curricular implications for approximately the last 40 years—are given in Table 1.2.

As shown in the table, special education students in the early 1960s typically were placed in self-contained classes for most of their school day and were educated under the assumption that a specialized curriculum was required to meet their unique educational needs. During the late 1960s, educators began to question this type of placement and the assumptions underlying it. In the 1970s and 1980s, a change occurred in the thinking regarding educational placements of students with special needs (i.e., resource and general class placements), as well as a growing conviction that special education students might benefit from selected aspects associated with the type of curriculum typically taught in general education classes. This idea prevailed into the 1990s and evolved to the point where education in inclusive classroom settings became the preferred option.

Determining the most effective educational setting for students with learning and behavior problems continues to challenge educators. Although the debate concerning full inclusion (all students learning in general education classrooms all the time) is far from over, the placement of students with learning and behavior problems into inclusive settings will continue to increase. What is also apparent, as noted by Fuchs and Fuchs (1994), is that special and general educators must redefine their relationship. It is beyond the scope of this book to undertake extended discussions on this debate; therefore, the reader is referred to Fuchs and Fuchs (1994), Hallahan and Kauffman (1995), Reynolds, Zetlin, and Wang (1993), and Stainback and Stainback (1996) for a more detailed discussion of inclusive education for these students.

The impact of inclusive education will be felt in a variety of ways in both special and general education classroom settings. Nowhere is the impact of the inclusion movement more pronounced than in the area of curricula and their implementation and adaptation. The increase in (a) the number of special learners who are educated in general education classes, and (b) the emphasis upon mandated curricula for all students highlights the need for educators to be able to adapt curricula competently. The current and projected educational placements and curricular requirements for students with special needs present a unique challenge to educators of these learners. As a result, educators must adapt or modify the curriculum for special learners while ensuring that these students follow

Table 1.2

Trends in Educational Placements of Special Education Students in Elementary and Secondary Schools

Stage	Period	Predominant Theme	Primary Placement(s)	Prevailing Thought Toward Education	Predominant View Toward Curriculum
I	Early 1960s	Separate special education was needed	Self-contained classroom	Students who could not benefit from general education would be best served in special classrooms	Specialized curriculum and techniques were needed to effectively educate individuals with disabilities
II	Late 1960s	Effectiveness of separate special classrooms was questioned	Self-contained classroom	Educators were questioning the practice and effects of educating students with disabilities in separate special classes	The need for special curriculum and techniques for many students with disabilities was being questioned
III	1970s	Education for many students with special needs does not have to occur in separate special classrooms	Resource rooms with some education in general education classrooms	Many learners may benefit from education in general education classrooms, requiring only some education in a special classroom	Selected aspects of the general education curriculum were appropriate for learners with special needs
IV	1980s	Students with special needs may be appropriately educated in general education classrooms	General education classrooms with some education in resource rooms	The least restrictive environment for many students termed disabled is education in the general education classroom	Many students may benefit from the general education curriculum if proper adaptations and modifications are provided
V	1990s	Students with disabilities should achieve full inclusion into general education	Full integration into general education services and classrooms	The education of all students with disabilities is best achieved in the general education setting	Continued expansion of integrated programs and curricula implemented in inclusive education settings

the mandated district or state curriculum. To do this successfully, teachers must know the general levels of influence upon curricula, current curricular trends, and views toward implementation of curricula for students with special learning needs.

Curriculum Defined

One of the first issues classroom teachers encounter in the overall teaching and learning process is that of defining the term *curriculum*. In general, how one defines this term relates directly to how one approaches it. Although a direct, perfect relationship between curricular approaches and definitions does not exist, there is considerable overlap. As a result, curricular definitions guide classroom teachers and other school-related personnel in their decision making concerning curricular components, implementation processes, and adaptations.

Numerous definitions of the term curriculum exist (e.g., Eisner, 1985; Walker & Soltis, 1992). These definitions typically fall along a continuum, with the highly specific and focused definitions at one end and the more general, all-inclusive ones at the other end. The former are viewed primarily as courses of study, whereas the latter include all or most events under the direction of the school. Definitions falling in the middle of the continuum represent compromises between the two.

Although these definitions continue to evolve, several educators, including curriculum specialists, define curriculum simply as the planned and guided learning experiences under the direction of the school. In an effort to focus and limit this definition, Eisner (1985) posited that these experiences should have intended educational outcomes. This is the idea of curriculum used throughout this book. Specific elements constituting a curriculum that are important to consider in the implementation and adaptation processes will be discussed in a subsequent section, and various conceptualizations of key components in the overall implementation process will be presented. However, different *types* of curricula do exist and must be considered in order to grasp fully the many issues that surround curriculum adaptations.

Curriculum Types

In addition to identifying and recognizing an operational definition of curriculum, teachers must also be cognizant of the different types of curricula that exist. Three types that are frequently mentioned are *explicit, hidden,* and *absent* (Eisner, 1985; Schubert, 1993). Hoover (1987) discussed the three types relative to the preparation of special educators.

Explicit curriculum refers to the formal and stated curriculum that teachers and students are expected to follow. The explicit curriculum is frequently outlined in the various curricular guides, which are usually ordered sequentially and span grades K through 12. This type of curriculum includes the specific goals and objectives for different subject areas such as reading, language, math, science, and social studies. The explicit curriculum is also found in publicized course listings; documented required content areas and teaching methods; or school catalogs made available to students, parents, and other community members. The "explicit curriculum is the published, advertised, and documented curriculum that schools say they are providing to students" (Hoover, 1987, p. 59).

Hidden curriculum refers to the actual curriculum implemented in the classroom—what students learn on a daily basis as teachers make inferences about the explicit curriculum they are required to teach (Klein, 1991). The hidden curriculum is found in the various practices, characteristics, or features that result from the decisions made by educators as the stated goals or objectives (i.e., explicit curriculum) are implemented. A hidden curriculum may sometimes negate important aspects of the explicit curriculum due to students learning unintentional outcomes. This happens because the explicit curriculum cannot account for all planned learning. The hidden curriculum includes interpretations made about explicit curricula related to implementation procedures and the emphasis different explicit curriculum aspects receive. For example, allowing a group of students to spend an entire month on one topic while allotting 1 week for study of another topic within the explicit curriculum represents hidden curricular issues. The different grouping situations within the classroom to implement explicit curricula also represents an example of a hidden curriculum. Other examples of hidden curricula include factors such as class structure or routines, selected academic or behavioral expectations, reward and reinforcement systems, selection and use of problem-solving techniques to study a required topic, different seating arrangements, and various types of acceleration and enrichment practices.

Absent curriculum refers to the curriculum we elect not to include in our schools or classrooms. This type of curriculum includes subject areas, content, teaching strategies, behavior management techniques, or classroom organizational dimensions that are excluded for various reasons. It is critical for teachers to be aware of absent curricula in their classrooms. Eisner (1985) wrote that what educators choose to exclude or not to teach may be just as important as what they elect to teach in their classrooms. As a result, "content to which students are not exposed, thinking abilities they are not required or encouraged to use . . . or behavior management methods that are not employed may all represent absent curriculum" (Hoover, 1987, p. 60).

Elements from explicit, hidden, and absent curricula operate continually in each classroom, sometimes complementing each other and at other times negating each other. This interaction is illustrated in Figure 1.2. The letter "I" in the figure identifies the various possibilities for curricular interactions:

- Explicit and Hidden

- Explicit and Absent

- Hidden and Absent

- Explicit, Hidden, and Absent

These interactions must be considered as teachers determine what curriculum adaptations are necessary. For example, in many situations the adaptations may include the addition of content or educational practices as a means to deal with absent curricula, along with adaptations to explicit or hidden curricula. In other situations, adaptations of hidden

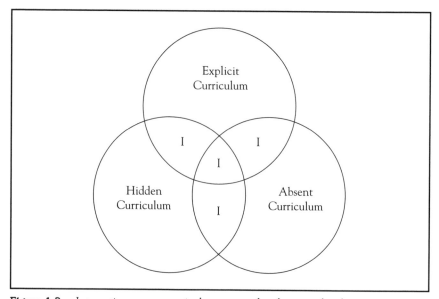

Figure 1.2. Interaction among curricular types at the classroom level.

curricula are required along with or instead of adaptations to the explicit curriculum. As the topic of curriculum adaptations is explored throughout this book, the reader should bear in mind that decisions concerning the types of curricula that require adaptations are just as important as selecting and implementing adaptation strategies, particularly as they relate to hidden and absent curricula.

Curricular Elements

Within the parameters of a more general definition of curriculum, specific elements need to be identified. Although a general conceptualization of curriculum is understood by most educators, the specific aspects or elements that constitute it are not as clearly apparent. As discussed previously, one of the major characteristics of the more general definitions of curriculum is that it includes more than just content (i.e., subject matter or materials within the classroom). This idea can be confusing, as the usual assumption is that curriculum refers to content. However, for the purposes of this book, four major elements are associated with the actual practice of implementing a curriculum:

- content
- instructional strategies
- classroom instructional settings
- student behaviors

To implement a curriculum effectively, including its adaptations, each of the four elements must be understood thoroughly. It is also important to realize that these elements:

- can act as individual elements within the total curriculum implementation process;
- interrelate with one another; and
- are responsive to individual student needs and abilities.

The essential elements in the total implementation process, and the interaction among curriculum adaptations in each of the four curricular elements are illustrated in Figure 1.3. As shown, the four major elements of content, instructional strategies, instructional settings, and student behaviors are illustrated as individual aspects within the total curriculum

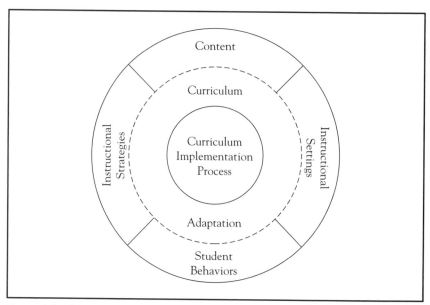

Figure 1.3. Integration among elements, adaptation, and implementation as related to a curriculum. *Note.* Adapted from *Classroom Management Through Curricular Adaptations: Educating Minority Handicapped Students* (p. 11), by J. J. Hoover and C. Collier, 1986, Boulder, CO: Hamilton Publications. Copyright 1986 by Hamilton Publications. Adapted with permission.

implementation process. The four elements are connected to the adaptation process. The dotted line that connects the elements with the adaptation process signifies the interrelationship among these areas. As the four elements are implemented and adapted, effective implementation of the total curriculum emerges.

In reference to each individual curricular element, *content* refers to the different academic skills or knowledge associated with each subject area. In today's K–12 educational institutions, this knowledge generally is taught through sequentially ordered programs or curricula that emphasize completion of prerequisite skills necessary to succeed in successive units of study or grades. The *instructional strategies* element includes the various techniques or methods used to assist students in acquiring content and managing behavior. Numerous teaching and behavior management techniques exist for implementing or adapting a curriculum; many of these are addressed in Chapter 2. The *instructional settings* element refers to the different settings found within a classroom, including small- or large-group situations, independent seatwork, and one-to-one instructional situations. The *student behaviors* element within the total curriculum refers to students' abilities to manage and control their own behaviors within a variety of learning situations and groupings found in the classroom.

Through reference to the three types of curricula relative to the four curricular elements, we are able to see that the explicit curriculum includes the content, instructional strategies, instructional settings, or management procedures that are stated, publicized, and outlined in the school's public information catalogs, handbooks, or curriculum guides. The hidden curriculum includes content, instructional strategies, instructional settings, and management procedures that, although not stated or explicitly outlined, are used regularly at the classroom level as the explicit curriculum demands are addressed. The absent curriculum refers to content, instructional strategies, instructional settings, or management procedures that could be included in the daily implementation of curricula but are not, for various reasons.

Each of the four curricular elements contributes to the overall implementation process. With few exceptions, the four elements reflect the total curriculum process and must be addressed as teachers make decisions concerning implementation or adaptation of curricula. Although these four elements represent distinct components within the total curriculum, the interrelationship among the elements provides the key to the successful implementation and adaptation of a curriculum.

Interrelationship Among Curricular Elements

Problems and inconsistencies in the classroom that inhibit effective implementation of a curriculum frequently result from difficulties related to a combination of certain curricular elements. Although problems limited to only one curricular element are sometimes encountered, students with learning and behavior problems generally experience simultaneous difficulties related to two or more elements. Regardless of which elements are problematic for a student with special needs, teachers typically concentrate their search for solutions on one element, failing to consider the interrelationships among the elements. Recognizing the possible interaction(s) can lead to a more comprehensive problem-solving process (see Figure 1.4).

As shown in the figure, the four elements appear along the outer borders. The center portion of the figure identifies the implementation process that is achieved through each of the four curricular elements. The areas within the figure describe interrelationships among curricular

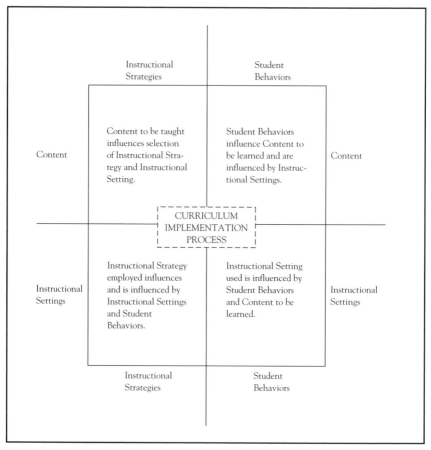

Figure 1.4.   Interrelationship among curricular elements in the curriculum implementation process.

elements. The following two situations illustrate examples of these interrelationships.

Interrelationship Among Elements: Situation 1

Tom is a fifth-grade student who is functioning academically at a second-grade level in reading and language. He attends a special education resource room on a daily basis for remedial work in reading and language instruction. In addition, he has difficulty working with other students, especially in small-group situations. Tom frequently hits other students while waiting to respond to questions or when others are responding to questions asked by the teacher. The teacher wishes to teach Tom some second-grade sight words. Several other students in the same class also need to learn the same sight words. The teacher chooses to present the sight words (content) on flash cards and asks Tom to pronounce each word verbally (instructional strategy) in a one-to-one situation (instructional setting). In this example, Tom's behavior influenced the instructional setting (i.e., one-to-one setting). In addition, the instructional strategy (i.e., flash-card presentation) was influenced by Tom's behavior as well as the content to be learned. If Tom was capable of working with others, a small-group situation might have been selected because other students in the class required work in the same content area.

However, suppose the teacher decides to present the words in a small-group setting that includes Tom. Because Tom has difficulty waiting his turn, the strategy of asking each student to respond one at a time to the sight words on flash cards may not be in Tom's best interest or that of the others in the group. Changing the instructional setting to a small group rather than a one-to-one situation means that the teacher also needs to change the instructional strategy to meet both Tom's needs and those of other students. Instead of showing the flash cards one at a time and asking each student to take turns responding, sight-word bingo might be played. In this game, all students must respond to each flash card by placing a check mark on the same sight word on their cards as shown on the flash card.

The interrelationship among elements is very evident in this situation. The selection of the small-group situation (i.e., instructional setting) directly influenced the instructional strategy. As the instructional setting element was altered for Tom, the instructional strategy also required change. Thus, the instructional setting influenced the instructional strategy and was influenced by student (Tom's) behaviors.

Interrelationship Among Elements: Situation 2

Mary is a sixth-grade student who is functioning academically in reading and math at about the fourth-grade level. She is an extremely shy, withdrawn student. Mary was appropriately placed into special education where she receives resource room assistance on a daily basis for work on academics and social/emotional development. Based upon this information, the teacher chooses to teach Mary interpersonal and social relationship skills (content) in small-group and one-to-one situations (instructional settings) through a peer-tutoring approach (instructional strategy). Work in the academic areas is completed on a one-to-one basis until Mary feels more comfortable working in group situations.

In this example, a student's behavior (i.e., Mary's behavior) influenced the selection of content (i.e., social skills development), the instructional setting (i.e., small-group, one-to-one), and the instructional strategy (i.e., peer tutoring). Moreover, the instructional strategy was influenced by the content selected and the instructional setting used.

As illustrated in the two examples, the interrelationship among curricular elements is evident even in the most basic types of implementation. These examples highlight the concept that implementation of a curriculum in any classroom involves a very complicated process of decision making in which the interrelationship among various curricular elements must be addressed when teachers consider curriculum adaptations. Efforts to minimize behavior problems or to increase learning may not succeed unless the interrelationship among curricular elements is considered in the process of selecting and implementing adaptations. Teachers may spend several weeks implementing an adaptation program that focuses on one particular element only to realize later that other factors also contribute to the presenting problem. If the interrelationship among two or more curricular elements is overlooked, efforts to improve learning or reduce behavior problems may be futile.

The decision to select, implement, change, modify, or adapt one curricular element relative to the other three elements is central to the success of curriculum adaptations. As one element is adapted, each of the other three must be considered in order to ascertain potential effects of the original adaptation. Careful consideration of these issues prior to the selection and implementation of curriculum adaptations increases successful outcomes.

Curricular Conceptions

Thus far this discussion has emphasized the importance of having an operational definition of curriculum, acknowledging the different types of curricula, and recognizing the major elements that constitute a curriculum in order to select and implement appropriate adaptations effectively. Teachers must also be cognizant of the critical influences of different orientations or philosophical positions associated with the operational definition of curriculum, which provides a basis for making curricular decisions. The influences of different curricular orientations are reflected in the operational definition a person such as a teacher follows and how he or she views different key aspects associated with the curriculum. Miller and Seller (1985) identified several aspects associated with a curriculum and its implementation relative to curricular conceptions. Five issues relevant to classroom teachers and other educators who implement curricula include the following:

- educational aims
- the learner
- the learning process
- the learning environment
- the role of the teacher

Constant interaction exists among the issues and teacher conceptions of them (see Figure 1.5). The curricular conceptions element is located in the central portion of the figure, with the five selected curricular issues located around it. Each educator possesses various conceptions of each

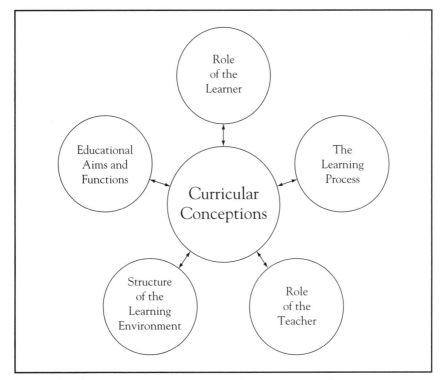

Figure 1.5.   Interactive process among curricular conceptions and issues.

Table 1.3
Conceptions of Curricular Issues

Issues	Conceptions
Educational aims and functions	Role of education is to "transmit" facts, skills, or values to students *versus* one of "dialogue" between the student and curriculum in which the student "reconstructs" knowledge through the process of dialogue.
Role of the learner	The learner is viewed as an "active" participant *versus* one who functions in a highly "passive" role.
The learning process	The learning process emphasizes the "inner life" of the learner *versus* change in the "external" behavior of the student.
Structure of the learning environment	The ideal learning environment is one that is "highly" structured *versus* a more open "loosely" structured learning situation.
Role of the teacher	The ideal situation is to take a strong teacher "directive" role *versus* one of a "facilitator" of student learning.

issue. Also depicted (by the arrows) is the constant interaction among the curricular conceptions element and the issues.

Curricular conceptions reflect different, often contrasting, viewpoints regarding the issues, examples of which are presented in Table 1.3. Less extreme possibilities exist between the two conceptual extremes presented in the "Conceptions" column in the table (e.g., active versus passive), and, according to Miller and Seller (1985), educators may "adhere to a cluster of two or three orientations to curriculum" (p. 5). It is beyond the scope of this book to explore the various orientations toward curricula that influence conceptions of the five issues identified. (The reader is referred to the various curriculum sources cited throughout this section for detailed discussions about this topic.)

Whether educators tend to adhere to single or multiple curricular orientations, it is critically important for them to develop an awareness of what their orientations are. This is important not only in understanding the overall curriculum process employed within the classroom, but also in clarifying further the decision-making process concerning the adaptation of one or more curricular elements. Teachers' views regarding each issue will reflect directly upon how they view potential curriculum adaptations.

They must realize that each of their conceptions is important in the over-all decision-making process regarding curriculum adaptations: The selection and use of curriculum adaptations are made within the parameters of how teachers view each of the five issues. This, coupled with the concepts of explicit, hidden, and absent curricula, assists teachers in further clarifying their own orientations toward the overall implementation process and subsequent curriculum adaptations.

Discussion Issues

1. Discuss recent educational issues and their impact upon the education of special education students.

2. Provide examples of explicit, hidden, and absent curricula for each of the four curricular elements.

3. Discuss or develop classroom situations in which the interrelationship among curricular elements is most evident.

4. Discuss how different orientations toward the five curricular issues outlined in this chapter may affect decisions related to curriculum adaptations.

Identifying Curriculum Adaptation Needs

2

Most classrooms include students who do not learn without some modifications or adaptations of the curriculum. All experienced educators have been in classroom situations where students were unable to learn through the traditional curriculum without some adaptations to content, teaching methods, groupings, or management systems. Hammill and Bartel (1995) suggested that teachers frequently encounter students who exhibit problems in various academic areas, and Gearheart, Weishahn, and Gearheart (1996) wrote that a considerable range in abilities is found among students in many classrooms. This wide range in abilities emphasizes the need to adapt one or more curricular elements in order to educate effectively all students with learning and behavior problems. This situation occurs with greater frequency in special education classes, especially in the increasing numbers of states and districts that require mandated curricula. For some students who experience difficulty in the overall curriculum process, adaptation of content only may be required; however, other students may require adaptations to instructional strategies and/or classroom instructional settings or modifications of student behaviors.

In Chapter 1 we discussed several areas associated with curricula and their implementation:

1. the three different types of curricula in continuous operation in each classroom;

2. an operational definition of curriculum that indicates the parameters of different types;

3. four individual elements constituting a curriculum that operate in integrative ways in the total implementation process; and

4. numerous curricular issues, each of which affects implementation directly or indirectly.

The primary purpose for addressing each of these aspects was to give the reader a knowledge foundation regarding curricula that would assist him or her in making more informed and effective decisions concerning necessary adaptations.

This chapter focuses on the selection and implementation of curriculum adaptations. A model for adapting one or more of the curricular elements discussed previously is depicted as a flowchart in Figure 2.1. This model, referred to as the Curriculum Adaptation Model, begins with forming a knowledge base that encompasses issues and skills related to the topics discussed in Chapter 1.

The Curriculum Adaptation Model illustrates the major components that constitute the overall adaptation process. Components include the

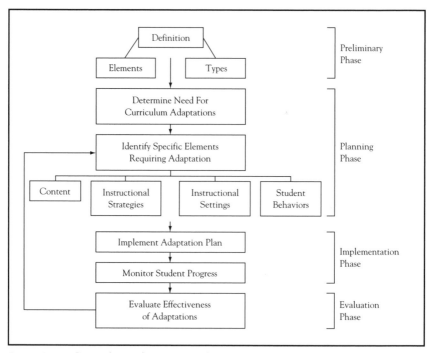

Figure 2.1. Curriculum Adaptation Model.

knowledge and skills necessary to: (a) determine the need for adapting curricular elements; (b) identify specific elements requiring adaptation; and (c) select and implement strategies that meet content, instructional strategy, instructional setting, and student behavior needs. These will be discussed in greater detail in this chapter, which includes a guide for determining curriculum adaptations and the interrelationship among the four curricular elements in the adaptation process. In addition, numerous teaching and behavior management techniques that may be selected and used to implement effective curriculum adaptations related to content, strategies, settings, and student behaviors are presented. These discussions begin with an examination of the need to adapt one or more of the curricular elements.

The Need for Curriculum Adaptations

As discussed in Chapter 1, many events have occurred in the past few *why* decades that have had an impact on schools and curricula. In today's classrooms, teachers are confronted with a variety of student needs and abilities. The need to adapt curricula increases as the variability of student abilities and learner characteristics increases.

Curriculum adaptation was defined as modifying or supplementing the curriculum to meet the needs of individual students. Up to this point in our discussion, general reasons have been presented regarding why curricula must be adapted. Specific reasons based upon student needs and abilities also exist and become readily apparent when one considers the similarities and differences among content, instructional strategy, instructional setting, and student behavior needs within a particular classroom (see Figure 2.2).

Because today's curricula are often mandated, specific content and objectives for students to study within each grade level are outlined. These content areas and objectives reflect experiences that the curriculum developers believe to be appropriate for students at each grade level. Success with the curriculum in a particular grade or course of study depends, to a great extent, upon the success one experiences with content and objectives from previous grades or courses of study. Within this structure, the need to adapt content of a curriculum is minimized when all students within a specific class or grouping require the same content. Conversely, the need for adapting content increases as students' differences in content needs increase. Although the content to be learned is

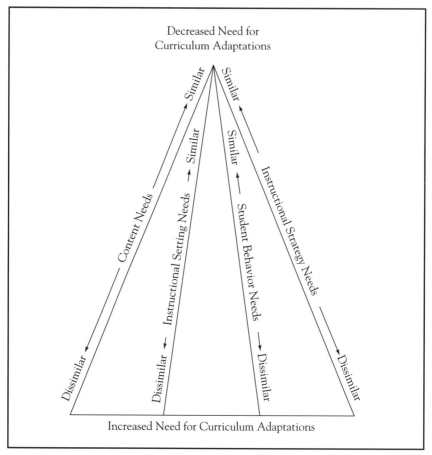

Figure 2.2.   Needs associated with curriculum adaptations.

an important consideration, teachers must address other curricular elements as well.

In addition to modifications of content, the curricular elements related to strategies, settings, and student behaviors may also require adaptations to meet students' special learning needs. The need for curriculum adaptations also increases as student needs related to the other elements of student behaviors, instructional strategies, and instructional settings in a class or group become dissimilar (see Figure 2.2). The need to adapt one or more elements as a result of dissimilar needs is currently widespread in many areas in U.S. schools.

Curriculum-Based Measurement and Assessment

Curriculum-based assessment (CBA) is an assessment method for determining specific instructional needs of students. Several researchers have discussed CBA and its various aspects (Choate et al., 1987; Fuchs & Deno, 1994; Hammill & Bartel, 1995; Polloway & Patton, 1996). Curriculum-based assessment is an alternative to formal, standardized tests and is typically conducted on an ongoing basis. According to Fuchs and Deno (1994), CBA has become a popular method due to its ability to provide teachers with specific information about a student's learning relative to what has been taught, and because of the local control maintained by school boards and other decision makers concerning the assessment of the selected school/district curricula.

In addition, Choate et al. (1987) identified several important reasons for using CBA, including the idea that CBA assists in:

1. determining what should be taught;
2. identifying appropriate teaching strategies;
3. facilitating frequent monitoring of student learning in an efficient and easy manner;
4. determining if specific learning styles or uses of learning strategies contribute to increased learning; and
5. providing a valid and reliable form of assessment due to its use of actual curricula completed by the students.

Although a variety of curriculum-based assessment methods exist, they share at least three common elements:

1. student proficiency is determined from the actual school and classroom curriculum;
2. the student assessment occurs over time; and
3. specific classroom instructional decisions result from the assessment information obtained (Fuchs & Deno, 1994).

An attractive feature of CBA is that it uses material directly related to the teaching and learning that occurs in the classroom. In addition, CBA has several advantages over formal standardized testing, as discussed by

Choate et al. (1987) and Mastropieri and Scruggs (1994). Curriculum-based assessment assists teachers in:

1. linking the scope and sequence of content with specific measures used in the assessment process;

2. completing a more direct assessment of student needs relative to the curricular elements;

3. implementing effective decisions concerning curricular issues at the classroom level;

4. modifying effectively most, if not all, curricular areas; and

5. determining specific skills that have been mastered as well as those that require priority emphasis for instruction.

A more rigorous form of classroom curriculum assessment is the set of standardized procedures for assessing student performance in a variety of content areas known as curriculum-based measurement (CBM) (Hammill & Bartel, 1995; Paulsen, 1997). Although CBM is able to connect the interrelated aspects of teaching, learning, and testing in a similar manner to that of CBA, it differs to some extent from the latter. According to Fuchs and Deno (1994), CBM has the following characteristics:

1. places emphasis on long-term instructional goals, whereas CBA focuses on a series of short-term objectives;

2. blends alternative assessment models with traditional models; and

3. relies on a standardized methodology, whereas CBA requires teacher-made measurement procedures.

Research has shown CBM to be as reliable and valid as most standardized norm-referenced tests (Hammill & Bartel, 1995). These important aspects (i.e., reliability and validity) allow educators to confidently use CBM as an alternative to standardized norm-referenced instruments to:

1. determine annual curriculum goals;

2. systematically assess samples of the curriculum and generate short, appropriate tests;

3. administer the short tests at regular intervals throughout the school year; and

4. use the results to adapt the curriculum as necessary.

According to Hammill and Bartel (1995), during curriculum-based measurement four specific items are identified and addressed, as illustrated in this adapted reading example:

Goal
Student will read 50 words per minute correctly with no more than five errors.

Materials
Randomly select pages from the student's reader.

Measurement Procedures
Student reads on preselected passage for 1 minute and teacher records the number of correct words and errors. This process repeats every week with a different passage read each time.

Evaluation/Record Keeping
Weekly performance data illustrating both the number of correct and incorrect words are kept for the student. These should be graphed for visual illustration.

The procedures illustrated in the above example provide reliable and valid information on student performance relative to a specific curricular content area. This method is particularly useful for identifying content area progress relative to specific instructional strategies as well as instructional settings. It complements CBA, which allows for detailed documentation in all four curricular areas of content, instructional strategies, instructional settings, and student behaviors.

Identifying Curricular Elements for Adaptation

Curriculum adaptations must become an integral part of daily teaching if each student's learning or behavior needs are to be addressed effectively at the classroom level. Because many learners with special needs are educated in both special and general education classrooms, special education teachers may be required to adapt curricula in their classrooms as well as assist general educators in adapting curricula in their classrooms. The curriculum adaptation issues discussed in this section

Educator: _____   Student: _____   Subject: _____

Strategy: _____

Class setting: _____

Place a check next to each item for which the student possesses sufficient abilities to work within the classroom relative to the identified subject, strategy, and setting.

Content Needs

- ❏ Sufficient reading level
- ❏ Necessary prerequisite skills
- ❏ Necessary prior experiences
- ❏ Sufficient language abilities
- ❏ Sufficient abstract thinking abilities
- ❏ Interest in subject area material
- ❏ Other:

Instructional Strategy Needs

- ❏ Motivated by strategy used
- ❏ Strategy generates active student participation
- ❏ Acquires information through strategy
- ❏ Understands strategy used
- ❏ Strategy holds student's attention to task
- ❏ Other:

(Continues)

Figure 2.3.   Curriculum Adaptation Quick Screen.

apply to both general and special education class placements. Special considerations that pertain to inclusion and curriculum adaptations are discussed in Chapter 3.

As previously discussed, CBA procedures help teachers to determine specific areas that need adaptation through assessment designed to identify and specify student needs regarding each of the four curricular elements. To assist in this area, two informal assessment devices for determining adaptation needs are presented. These are best used in conjunction with each other and with other appropriate classroom-level assessments. The *Curriculum Adaptation Quick Screen* (see Figure 2.3) provides a means to quickly identify one or more curricular elements that

Instructional Setting Needs

❏ Able to attend to task within type of setting used
❏ Able to work independently when necessary
❏ Possesses appropriate peer interaction skills for type of setting used
❏ Acquires information easily through setting used
❏ Participates freely in setting
❏ Completes assignments within setting used
❏ Other:

Student Behaviors

❏ Maintains self-control
❏ Completes assigned tasks on time
❏ Is responsible for own actions
❏ Uses effective self-management techniques
❏ Uses study and learning strategies effectively
❏ Exhibits appropriate behaviors for type of instructional setting used
❏ Other:

Summary of Curriculum Adaptation Needs

Content _____

_____

Instructional Strategy _____

_____

Instructional Setting _____

_____

Student Behaviors _____

_____

Figure 2.3.   Continued.

may require adaptation. The second is the *Guide for Curricular Adaptations* (see Figure 2.4 on page 29), which provides for a more detailed assessment in the four curriculum areas.

The *Curriculum Adaptation Quick Screen* includes information related to each of the four curricular elements. As shown, the screen is an informational device that provides several statements reflective of skills and abilities necessary to function within each of the four curricular elements. The guide is certainly not all-inclusive; rather, it contains several key components associated with each curricular element, with space provided for other needs not listed. To complete the screen, the teacher places a check next to each item that reflects skills and abilities possessed by the student or occurrences specific to the student's learning relative to an identified subject area. This may be completed based on observations of and discussions with the student, curriculum-based assessment data, and a review of the student's completed work. Those curricular elements receiving few checks may be problem areas for the student and may require adaptations or modifications to existing practices, settings, or content. Conversely, those areas receiving many checks are probably not potential problem areas for the student, indicating less of a need for adaptations relative to the specific content area. This guide provides the teacher with general information regarding curricular elements that appear to need modifications or adaptations to meet individual learning and behavior needs.

Once the Quick Screen has been completed and the need for adaptations has been determined, a more detailed assessment should be undertaken. One example is the *Guide for Curricular Adaptations*. It further delineates specific needs within each of the four curricular elements.

The Guide, developed within the general framework of CBA, addresses issues related specifically to daily curricular implementation. It also assists decision making related to the selection of teaching techniques, behavior management tactics, and student strategies for adapting one or more of the curricular elements.

The *Guide for Curricular Adaptations* can assist teachers in determining which curricular elements need adaptation once a problem has been identified. The sample guide shown in Figure 2.4 has been completed for illustrative purposes.

The Guide is composed of three sections. In Section I, classroom and instructional aspects specific to situations in which the student experiences difficulty are documented. These include student expectations during the instructional activity and the reason a concern exists in that particular situation. Section I also contains a general description that pertains to each curricular element. This information helps to clarify the existing structure and practices of the learning situation.

The information provided in Section I serves as a basis for completing the next section. In Section II, a question-and-answer narrative format is used to address issues related to the four curricular elements. In this section, attempts are made to further clarify student needs and abilities within a particular instructional situation as described in Section I. After

---

Student: Juan   Subject Area: Social Studies

Date: 10-10-86   Grade: 5

Length of Instructional Period: 40 minutes

I. Briefly describe the classroom situation and task in question:

   Content area addressed during this instructional period:
American History

   Instructional Strategy(s) used during this instruction:
Lecture and Discussion

   Instructional Setting(s) used during this instruction:
Large Group

   Student Behaviors exhibited during this instruction:
Makes tapping noises, looks around room

   Expectation of student during instruction:
Record notes, participate in discussions

   Reason for concern:
Lack of participation, poor grades on weekly tests

II. Respond to each curricular item relative to the described situation:

  A. Content

     1. Does student possess sufficient reading level to complete activity?
Yes, Juan reads at a fifth-grade level in English (L2) and Spanish (L1)

     2. Has student mastered previous objectives and skills necessary to complete activity?
Yes, successfully completed pretests

     3. Does student possess sufficient language skills, cultural background knowledge, and experiences to comprehend the concepts associated with the instruction?
Yes, speaks Spanish fluently, speaks and understands English similar to others in class, has been in this school/community since the first grade

    Summary of content needs:
Juan possesses sufficient reading level, prerequisite skills, experience, and language background to complete activity

(Continues)

Figure 2.4.   Guide for Curricular Adaptations. *Note.* From *Classroom Management Through Curricular Adaptations: Educating Minority Handicapped Students* (pp. 39–41), by J. J. Hoover and C. Collier, 1986, Boulder, CO: Hamilton Publications. Copyright 1986 by Hamilton Publications. Reprinted with permission.

B. Instructional Strategies

1. Does selected strategy(s) provide sufficient motivation to student?
   Juan appears to pay attention about half the period

2. Does selected strategy(s) generate active student participation?
   Juan rarely participates in discussions and records only a few notes

3. Under what conditions is the selected strategy(s) effective for the student?
   When the lecture is supplemented with frequent discussions

4. To what extent does the student learn through selected strategy(s)?
   Juan has not learned the material in this unit of study

   Summary of Instructional Strategy needs:
   Lecturing does not appear to motivate Juan or facilitate effective learning

C. Instructional Setting (one or more may apply to the specific situation being assessed)

1. To what extent is the student capable of working independently?

2. To what extent is the student capable of working in small-group situations with direct teacher supervision?
   Juan frequently participates in most large-group activities during Social Studies

3. To what extent is the student capable of working in large-group situations?

4. To what extent is the student capable of working cooperatively with one or two students without constant direct teacher supervision?

   Summary of Instructional Setting needs:
   Juan is usually capable of working and learning in large-group situations

D. Student Behaviors

1. What appropriate behaviors does the student exhibit during the instruction?
   For the most part Juan appears to pay attention except when looking around the room

2. What inappropriate behaviors does the student exhibit during the instruction?
   Frequently looks around the room and taps pencil on desk

(Continues)

Figure 2.4. Continued.

3. During the instruction, how long does the student attend to the task at hand prior to exhibiting off-task behavior? Length of time before returning to task?
5-10 minutes prior to tapping or looking around, Returns to task within a couple of minutes

4. How much of the entire instructional time is engaged in on-task behavior? Off-task behavior?
50%-60% on-task   40%-50% off-task

5. What self-management techniques does the student use to manage own behavior and attend to the task at hand?
Juan is capable of returning to the task without teacher direction

Summary of Student Behavior needs:
Juan possesses some self-control abilities. He frequently looks around the classroom and occasionally taps his pencil on his desk

III. Prioritize curricular elements requiring adaptation:

Curricular Elements	Adaptation Priority			
	High	Medium	Low	Further Clarification
Content			X	
Instructional Strategy	X			
Instructional Setting			X	
Student Behaviors		X		

Hypothesis for adaptations: Present Juan with an outline of topics that will be covered during the lecture prior to beginning the lecture. Assign Juan a bilingual peer tutor to answer questions he may have about the content. Periodically stop lecture and ask students (including Juan) to summarize the content to that point. A self-monitoring program for the tapping noises and looking around may be developed to reduce off-task behaviors if adaptations to the strategy are ineffective.

Figure 2.4. Continued.

the student has completed the responses to each curricular element, a brief statement is generated summarizing those responses.

In Section III, a chart is provided for recording and prioritizing curriculum adaptation needs based upon the results from the first two sections. The need to adapt one or more elements of the curriculum relates to the discrepancy between what the student is required to learn and what he or she actually learns during the instructional activity. Within the curricular element of content, the extent to which the student lacks sufficient reading level, mastery of prerequisite skills, and language abilities associated with the instructional activity reflects the potential need to adapt the content. The extent to which the instructional activity fails to motivate or generate active student participation reflects the need to adapt the instructional strategy.

Similarly, if the student lacks the capability to work within a group or independently, there exists a potential need to adapt the instructional setting. If the student exhibits inappropriate or off-task behaviors and the general inability to manage personal behavior within an instructional activity, it may be necessary to modify the behaviors that focus specifically on self-control. In any attempt to formulate a hypothesis concerning a proper course of action, prioritizing the need to adapt each particular curricular element helps to clarify the interrelationship among all the elements.

After the teacher or other professional has completed the Guide, further clarification regarding the need for curriculum adaptation may be necessary. If further assessment is not necessary and adaptations appear warranted, the teacher documents a hypothesis concerning the nature and type of required adaptations.

In the example in Figure 2.4, the student, Juan, possesses the ability to speak in both English and Spanish; however, the instructional strategy may not motivate him or generate his active participation, and he engages in frequent off-task behavior. Juan appears to possess sufficient prerequisite skills to learn the content, and the classroom instructional setting does not appear to be a major contributing factor to the problem. Therefore, only the instructional strategy or Juan's behaviors appear to require modifications. The hypothesis for curriculum adaptations in this situation initially should address adapting the instructional strategy followed by modifying Juan's behaviors to improve self-control. Depending upon the student and situation, the teacher may simultaneously undertake modifications of both the instructional strategy and student behaviors. In Juan's case the problem does not appear to be related to the content and instructional setting, and these elements are not adapted at this time. The teacher's hypothesis describes possible alternatives for implementing adaptations that address curricular needs.

As shown in this example, an apparently simple problem may be associated with two of the four curricular elements. Although some extra time is necessary to complete the Guide, its use may assist in maximizing effective selection and implementation of curriculum adaptations. As the adaptations are implemented, actual student performance provides the basis for the final decisions concerning the continued need for and effectiveness of the adaptations. Within individual classrooms, curriculum adaptations become a continuous process for some students with special learning needs.

The *Guide for Curricular Adaptations* should be completed with an individual student when the teacher determines that the student is experiencing problems with one or more elements within the total curriculum implementation process. Its use is appropriate for both special and general education classes and can be extremely helpful for communicating information about a student's needs. If several instructional periods within the school day are affected (e.g., small reading group, language arts class, independent seatwork during math), the Guide should be completed for each instructional area. It is designed so that general questions related to each of the four curricular elements are asked of the student. Additional questions and related issues may arise and be explored as the teacher completes the Guide.

Interrelationship Among Elements

As emphasized, it is often impossible to implement a curriculum effectively for students with special learning needs without some modification or change to the existing curriculum used with other students in the classroom. In essence, curriculum adaptations are necessary to achieve the most effective curriculum implementation process. This process, which consists of four interrelated elements, is illustrated in Figure 2.5. Just as one element influences other elements, adaptations in one curricular area may affect or be affected by one or more of the other curricular areas.

For example, in one situation, content as well as instructional strategies may require adaptations. In another situation, the classroom instructional setting may require adaptations to accommodate a specific instructional strategy. In addition, management strategies may require adaptations to facilitate greater self-control among students within particular instructional settings. The interrelationship among curricular elements emphasizes the need to consider the potential effects of adaptations upon the other elements. The successful adaptation of curricular elements may rest, to a great extent, on the decisions made regarding these effects. Curriculum adaptations may not succeed without considering all aspects within the total process.

Figure 2.5.   Interrelationship among curricular elements in curriculum adaptation. *Note.* Adapted from *Classroom Management Through Curricular Adaptations: Educating Minority Handicapped Students* (p. 47), by J. J. Hoover and C. Collier, 1986, Boulder, CO: Hamilton Publications. Copyright 1986 by Hamilton Publications. Adapted with permission.

Types of Curricula and the Adaptation Process

When considering potential adaptations and the interrelationship among the four curricular elements, the teacher must also address issues related to the different types of curricula (i.e., explicit, hidden, absent). In some situations the explicit curriculum may require adaptations. This is most evident when adaptation or modification of content or stated objectives is needed. However, problems related to any of the four curricular elements may result from: (a) failure to employ the use of a specific instructional strategy, classroom instructional setting, or management strategy (i.e., absent curriculum), or (b) ineffective use of a particular instructional strategy, instructional setting, or management technique when implementing a required curriculum or facilitating self-control with an individual or group of learners (i.e., a hidden curriculum).

In the first situation, the *addition* of a particular instructional strategy, setting, or management technique may be the necessary form of curriculum adaptation. In the second situation, however, changes or modifications of current classroom practices may be the required form of adaptation. Curriculum adaptations may, therefore, involve modifications and/or additions to existing content, instructional strategies, classroom instructional settings, or management techniques to facilitate learning content or to maintain greater self-control. Making adaptations related to the explicit, absent, and hidden curricula allows teachers to experience greater success with students who have special learning needs.

Curriculum Adaptation and Learning Style Preferences

Learning styles are characteristic ways in which students respond to instruction (Hoover, 1993) and relate to the successful implementation of curriculum adaptations. Learning styles vary across individuals, and many learners tend to use, emphasize, and overlearn a few select learning responses or strategies. Curriculum adaptation needs may be best met if students use different learning strategies as various situations dictate. Determining which learning strategies may be most appropriate for specific students begins with the identification of a student's learning style preferences. (See Table 2.1 for an overview of key learning style preferences.)

In order to understand learning styles, teachers must identify associated cognitive styles, such as field, tolerance, tempo, categorization, persistence, anxiety, and locus of control.

1. *Field*: Refers to how students view an experience, idea, or situation (i.e., view the collective whole rather than an emphasis on discrete or separate parts);

2. *Tolerance*: The willingness of students to accept experiences that vary significantly from common, everyday reality;

Table 2.1
Cognitive Styles and Related Learning Strategies

Style	Tendencies	Learning Strategies
Field	Independent Tendency to see everything as elements making up a whole; emphasis upon the parts and not the whole. Sensitive Tendency to see the whole; difficulty separating the whole from its parts.	Evaluation Organization
Tolerance	High tolerance Tendency to accept experiences that vary markedly from the ordinary or even from reality or the truth. Low tolerance Tendency to show a preference for conventional ideas and reality.	Analogy Coping Rehearsal
Tempo	Reflective Tendency to take more time and generate more effort to provide appropriate responses. Impulsive Tendency to give first answer that comes to mind even if frequently wrong or inappropriate.	Active processing Evaluation Rehearsal
Categorization	Broad Tendency to include many items in a category and lessen the risk of leaving something out. Narrow Tendency to exclude doubtful items and lessen the probability of including something that doesn't belong.	Analogy Evaluation Organization

(Continues)

Table **2.1** *Continued*

Style	Tendencies	Learning Strategies
Persistence	High Tendency to work until the task has been completed; seeks any necessary help.	Active processing Coping Evaluation
	Low Tendency to short attention; inability to work on a task for any length of time.	
Anxiety	High Tendency to perform less well when challenged by a difficult task.	Coping Evaluation
	Low Tendency to perform better when challenged by a difficult task.	
Locus of control	Internal Tendency to think of oneself as responsible for own behavior.	Active processing Coping Evaluation
	External Tendency to see circumstances as beyond one's control; luck or others are seen as responsible for one's behavior.	

3. *Tempo:* Aspects of cognitive tempo pertain to the speed and adequacy of hypothesis formation and information processing (i.e., reflective or impulsive);

4. *Categorization:* The ways in which students tend to group items, ranging from broad to narrow categorizations;

5. *Persistence:* Variations in the willingness of students to work beyond required time limits, withstand discomfort, and persist in efforts to complete tasks;

6. *Anxiety:* The level of anxiety and apprehension experienced by students in learning situations; and

7. *Locus of Control:* Whether students tend to attribute behavior and achievement to internal or external factors.

As shown in Table 2.1, each of these cognitive styles has associated learning strategies that can be used by teachers to better understand themselves and their students (Good & Brophy, 1990). Of specific importance to the classroom teacher is the identification of learning styles, which in turn will guide curriculum adaptation decisions. The learning styles associated with each cognitive style may be viewed as two extremes, with most students exhibiting a tendency toward one or the other extreme; however, in some students, a balance in the use of learning styles may be found.

The *Guide for Identifying Learning Styles* is given in Figure 2.6. This guide lists each cognitive style along with the two extreme learning style tendencies. To complete the Guide, the teacher places a check next to the specific learning style tendency that is most characteristic of the student. If the student exhibits a balanced emphasis for any set of learning styles, the balanced tendency should be checked. Specific learning style preferences should be summarized at the end of the Guide and may be referred to when the teacher is selecting curriculum adaptation strategies for that student. Information needed to complete the Guide should be obtained through observations and discussions with the student about ways he or she approaches different situations and tasks. For more detailed information about these cognitive learning styles, the reader is referred to Hoover (1993) and Collier and Hoover (1987).

As with the *Guide for Curricular Adaptations*, this guide should be completed by both special and general education teachers. The results should be compared to ensure consistent delivery of instruction in both settings as curriculum adaptations are selected and implemented.

Discussion Issues

1. Discuss the need for adapting curricular elements and outline a process that may be followed to determine which elements require adaptations.

2. Discuss the interrelationships among curricular elements in the implementation process and provide examples that demonstrate why consideration of these interrelationships is important to the selection and implementation of curriculum adaptations.

3. Provide examples that illustrate adaptations to explicit, hidden, and absent curricula.

4. Explain why cognitive learning styles must be considered to effectively implement curriculum adaptations.

Educator:_____ Student:_____

For each set of learning styles, check the *One* that most accurately reflects the student's preferred style of learning or approach to tasks.

Field

- ❏ Independent—Emphasizes parts, not the whole
- ❏ Sensitive—Emphasizes the whole; difficulty separating whole from its parts
- ❏ Balance—Independent/sensitive

Tempo

- ❏ Reflective—Takes much time and effort to generate appropriate responses
- ❏ Impulsive—Typically provides the first response that comes to mind in a random or quick manner
- ❏ Balance—Reflective/impulsive

Categorization

- ❏ Broad—Includes many items when categorizing to lessen the potential of omitting items that belong, which often results in the inclusion of items that do not belong
- ❏ Narrow—Excludes some items when categorizing to lessen the potential to include something that does not belong
- ❏ Balance—Broad/narrow

Locus of Control

- ❏ Internal—Attributes successes/failures to own efforts; responsible for own actions
- ❏ External—Attributes successes/failures to luck, ease of task, other people, or circumstances controlled by others
- ❏ Balance—Internal/external

Tolerance

- ❏ High—Very imaginative, prefers experiences that vary markedly from the ordinary
- ❏ Low—Prefers conventional ideas, with a tendency to conform in most situations
- ❏ Balance—High/low

(Continues)

Figure 2.6.   The Guide for Identifying Learning Styles.

Persistence

- ❏ High—Frequently works until task is complete, seeking any necessary assistance
- ❏ Low—Short attention to task, gives up quickly if task takes too long
- ❏ Balance—High/low

Anxiety

- ❏ High—Performs less well in challenging situations and does not like pressure
- ❏ Low—Performs well when challenged, enjoys taking risks and likes pressure
- ❏ Balance—High/low

Summary of Learning Style Preferences

Summarize the responses by placing an **X** in the appropriate learning style preference row for each cognitive style.

Preference	Field	Tempo	Categ.	Locus	Toler.	Pers.	Anx.
Independent							
Sensitive							
Balance							
Reflective							
Impulsive							
Balance							
Broad							
Narrow							
Balance							
Internal							
External							
Balance							
High							
Low							
Balance							

Figure 2.6.   Continued.

Implementing Curriculum Adaptations

3

. . . .

Once teachers have identified the specific curricular needs of their students and which curriculum adaptations to make, they are confronted with the challenge of actually implementing these adaptations. Effective implementation begins with the selection of teaching and behavior management techniques to address the needs associated with the curricular elements. A variety of intervention techniques for adapting curriculum effectively are presented in this section, along with student learning and study strategies. This chapter begins with specific adaptation issues related to each of the four curricular elements—content, instructional strategies, instructional settings, and student behaviors.

General Implementation Guidelines

Adapting Content

The need to adapt content has become more of an issue for teachers of students with special needs due to increased emphasis upon state- or district-mandated curricula in which the objectives related to subject material that students must be taught are already outlined for teachers. As a result, teachers are responsible for teaching required content; however, adapting that content is frequently necessary to meet the needs of special learners.

Mastropieri and Scruggs (1994) recommended several general strategies for teachers to follow to maximize the coverage of required content:

1. identify the scope and sequence of required content;

2. estimate the amount of time required to teach the content for the entire school year;

3. monitor progress and adjust the pace of the presentation of the content accordingly;

4. provide ongoing reviews of previously acquired content; and

5. make certain that instructional activities are related to the content the student must learn.

Knowledge acquisition is not the only focus of curriculum at the classroom level; it typically serves as a foundation for content presented in subsequent grades or courses of study. Because most content is dictated by mandates, adaptations in this area often focus on the rate at which the teacher presents the content. According to Mastropieri and Scruggs (1994), well-paced instruction allows students to cover sufficient content to meet necessary instructional goals. Effective pacing ensures that students with special learning needs have sufficient opportunity to acquire and maintain content in special and general education classes.

Another adaptation that is often necessary when teaching prescribed content is addressing reading levels by simplifying the task. Through this technique, elements of the required material are reworded to meet individual students' reading levels. This may be accomplished in the following manner:

> Place plastic transparency sheets over the pages of material the student must read. Read through the material and, with a dark-color, fine-point marker, cross out the more difficult words. Using a different colored marker, write simpler synonyms for the more difficult words. These may be written above the marked-out words or in the margin next to the difficult words. Instruct the student to read the rewritten words instead of the marked-out words as he or she reads through the selection. This process may also be used to rewrite selected phrases in reading material.

The adaptation to content described in the above example allows students to read grade-level material at a level commensurate with their individual reading abilities. The transparencies may be saved and stored for future use with other students.

The simplification of content, along with appropriate pacing of required subject material, allows teachers of students with special learning needs to implement content more effectively. Because much of the decisions concerning what to teach have already been made for teachers, adaptations to content must be considered in terms of established district guidelines and the instructional strategies necessary to teach the content.

Adapting Instructional Strategies

Many adaptation efforts involve changes reflecting the instructional strategy needs of students. The techniques discussed in this chapter may be used to adapt instructional strategies either by including a new technique or by modifying an existing one at the classroom level. Adaptations to instructional strategies should reflect cues and reinforcements appropriate for the learner as well as motivation of and relevance to students. In addition, some instructional strategies may distract students while others may reduce external stimuli; this must be considered as teachers select adaptations to these strategies.

The teacher must consider several important factors when selecting strategies for adapting a curriculum. Most importantly, the instructional strategy must allow students to succeed with the task at hand. Prior educational successes, acquired prerequisite skills, current language skills, and the difficulty of material are important factors that must be considered prior to selecting and implementing adaptations to instructional strategies. Mastropieri and Scruggs (1994) identified adaptations to instructional strategies related to content implementation or to the management of behavior to include (a) clarifying goals, (b) using a step-by-step presentation, (c) modeling the procedures, and (d) monitoring student understanding and adjusting the presentation accordingly.

Regarding the clarification of goals, the major points to be covered in a lesson or activity should be outlined initially to students to ensure that they understand the task. These points should be covered separately using language and appropriate examples related to students' levels of learning. The step-by-step presentation is necessary to ensure that students are given a clear and organized lesson. Teacher modeling of the skill also assists in the process. Finally, teachers must monitor student responses continually and adjust the presentation as necessary. Although predicting the potentially complex segments of a lesson and adjusting the presentation accordingly prior to delivery are highly desirable, it is not always possible to anticipate all potential problems. To ensure student success, the teacher must be aware of these variables and make adjustments in a flexible manner while the presentation is being delivered (Mastropieri & Scruggs, 1994).

These elements, although important to learning new material, are also applicable to most situations where adaptations to a curriculum are necessary. The overall purpose for using a desired strategy must be determined prior to selecting it to use as an adaptation. Consideration of the four elements outlined previously will assist teachers in clarifying which techniques should be employed as adaptations. In addition, these elements provide one process to follow as instructional strategies are adapted to ensure a clear presentation. The techniques outlined in this chapter offer information and examples concerning desired outcomes for using each strategy. This information, along with the four steps described previously, gives students structured and varied opportunities to acquire and maintain knowledge and skills related to content and self-management.

Adapting Instructional Settings

Within the total curriculum implementation process, another important element that often requires adaptation is the instructional setting. Gleockler and Simpson (1988) identified several elements to consider when implementing instruction and subsequent adaptations to improve self-management of behavior or mastery of content. Each of these relates directly or indirectly to the types of groupings within the classroom (e.g., one-to-one, small group, large group, independent seatwork). Some elements to consider include:

- seating arrangements and use of study carrels;
- organization of different learning areas within the classroom;
- grouping arrangements;
- overall organization for delivering different types of instruction;
- flexibility in groupings based upon learning experiences provided; and
- general climate conducive to positive learning, quality time on task, and effective interactions.

The selection of the classroom instructional setting requires careful thought. Many instructional strategies can be employed successfully in different instructional settings, and the same content may be effectively taught in various settings.

Although a setting may be influenced by content or instructional strategies, the latter do not lead automatically to a predetermined instructional setting. For example, although the lecture approach typically is used with larger groups of students, it could also be used effectively with small groups. The instructional setting used on a daily basis in the classroom is *influenced* by the selection of content or an instructional strategy, not *dictated* by these selections. The teacher must consider several factors when choosing the most appropriate classroom instructional setting for students with special learning needs: The setting must (a) show the students that they are expected to manage their own behaviors, (b) provide a forum that minimizes their risk for failure, and (c) foster the message that students are expected to complete the task.

The student's prior educational successes related to different grouping situations, the difficulty of the material or assignment in question, the time required to complete the assigned task, the need for direct teacher–student or student–student interaction, and the appropriateness of a setting for implementing a particular strategy all influence the selection of a classroom instructional setting for any one particular assignment. The teacher can determine the best possible setting and use it effectively to assist learners in managing behavior and acquiring content-related skills by carefully considering these factors.

Modifying Student Behaviors

The curriculum element of student behaviors pertains to the learners' abilities to maintain and manage their own behaviors. The inability to do so often presents the greatest challenge to teachers of students with learning and behavior problems. Deficits in this area of curriculum management affect decisions related to the selection of classroom instructional settings, instructional strategies, and, to some extent, the type of content to be learned. *In other words, it is important for teachers to ensure that these other elements contribute to student management of behaviors.* The inability to control behavior may be linked directly to specific content (e.g., reading, math, science), specific types of instructional strategies (e.g., lecture, role playing), or a particular instructional setting (e.g., independent seatwork, small group). Careful consideration of student behaviors in the decision-making process regarding content, strategies, and settings will prove beneficial to both students and teachers.

Effective self-management of student behaviors assists learners in reducing the time necessary to complete tasks and in facilitating independent learning. Several programs for self-control or self-management exist (e.g., Fagen, Long, & Stevens, 1975; Workman & Katz, 1995), and the reader is referred to these sources for a complete description of the programs.

However, in general, success with student self-management programs through modifications of student behaviors increases as the teacher:

1. ensures that students are familiar with curricular expectations related to different tasks;

2. assists students in setting realistic and attainable goals in self-management;

3. implements curricular expectations in a consistent manner; and

4. allows sufficient time for a self-management program to be attempted and tested (Hoover & Patton, 1995).

Adaptation Strategies

Use of the following teaching, student learning, and student study strategies provides students with various opportunities to effectively meet their curriculum adaptation needs in both special and general education settings. Specific issues related to the collaboration necessary between special and general education teachers are discussed in the next chapter.

Teaching Strategies

There are a variety of teaching strategies, and several of these are presented in this section. The strategies presented here are appropriate for use when adaptations to content, instructional strategies, instructional settings, or student behaviors are necessary. These strategies reflect behavior management needs of students as well as content and classroom grouping needs related to various subject areas. They are appropriate for elementary or secondary students who have learning or behavior problems, whether taught in general or special education classrooms. Effectively meeting individual needs through curriculum adaptations may be facilitated through classroom use of these teaching strategies.

The strategies covered in this section were developed from information found in Friend and Bursuck (1996), Gearheart et al. (1996), Lewis and Doorlag (1995), Mercer and Mercer (1993), Polloway and Patton (1996), Salend (1994), Smith, Polloway, Patton, and Dowdy (1995), and Wood (1993). The format of each teaching strategy includes a brief description, major advantage(s), example(s), suggested uses, and special considerations for use in general education settings. The strategies are not presented in order of importance, as all are appropriate for implementing curriculum adaptations, depending on the circumstances (i.e., individual student academic learning style needs and abilities). For this reason, the strategies are not listed in any particular order.

Teaching Strategy: Contingency Contracting

Description

A verbal or written agreement is made between the teacher and the student outlining specific tasks, rewards, or consequences surrounding an assignment.

Advantage

This strategy helps students to specifically identify and be held account-able for their responsibilities regarding an assignment, including rewards and consequences.

Example

Document in writing that the student will remain seated during independent seatwork time without disturbing classmates. Student will receive 10 minutes of time to complete an activity of his or her choice in the library upon completion of the independent time.

Suggested Uses

This strategy should be used to help students complete various educational tasks. It is particularly appropriate when the recording of procedures and rewards helps a student to remain on task and to complete work. It may also be used to help students learn how to better monitor their time.

Inclusive Considerations

Mainstreamed students may benefit from this strategy while the teacher is engaged in working with other students, such as during reading or math times, or during other times when the teacher is not immediately available to the learner.

Teaching Strategy: Providing Choices

Description

The learner is given two or more options from which to select in order to complete an assignment.

Advantages

This strategy may assist in reducing fears associated with various assign-ments or types of tasks or may alleviate problems associated with teacher–student power struggles.

Example

Offer two different math papers, both of which address the same objective you wish the student to meet. Allow the learner to select and complete one of the papers for the assignment.

Suggested Uses

Giving students choices within structured situations helps them to become more responsible for their own education.

Inclusive Considerations

The teacher should ensure that the student knows exactly what the choices are and that he or she will be held accountable for whatever choice is made.

Teaching Strategy: Role Playing

Description

Situations are developed in which various roles may be acted out by students, based upon their perceptions about how they believe their characters may act.

Advantage

This strategy gives students an opportunity to experience different situa-tions from various vantage points in a safe and nonthreatening manner.

Example

Identify a social issue of specific relevance to a group of students. Assign roles to be played, act out the issue, and discuss the situation. After the discussion, have students switch roles and reenact the situation, followed by further discussion.

Suggested Uses

This strategy is particularly appropriate for helping students to confront issues they wish to avoid or fail to realize.

Inclusive Considerations

Role play may help mainstreamed students and others to become better accustomed to a new classroom or group of people. It should be considered as a way to reduce stigma often associated with the skills and needs of mainstreamed students.

Teaching Strategy: Student Input into Curriculum Decisions

Description

The learner is allowed to provide ideas and suggestions for selected daily curricular activities, keeping within the general parameters of the required elements.

Advantage

Students who are allowed to provide input into their education have greater ownership and may be more motivated to complete assignments.

Example

Allow students to select the manner in which they will present research on a specific topic (e.g., written report, oral presentation, video presentation).

Suggested Uses

This strategy should be used during the initial planning stages of units or courses of study and should be structured in ways that allow students to participate actively in the planning of various activities.

Inclusive Considerations

The teacher should make sure that students are aware of the parameters within which input may be provided and that their input is valued through use of their suggestions in curriculum implementation.

Teaching Strategy: Success Through Challenges

Description

This strategy emphasizes the need to provide students with successful experiences while simultaneously ensuring that assigned tasks are challenging.

Advantage

Successful completion of various educational tasks improves a student's self-confidence and self-perception, which in turn may facilitate continued cooperation and interest in learning.

Example

Reduce the difficulty level of an assignment and gradually increase to more difficult tasks in small, sequential steps as the student succeeds with each task.

Suggested Uses

This strategy is essential for students who are reluctant to learn or cannot seem to complete assignments.

Inclusive Considerations

Successful completion of tasks that are challenging to the student in a mainstreamed classroom is essential to ensure future progress toward educational goals.

Teaching Strategy: Shortened Assignments

Description

Students are provided with shortened versions of specific assignments, or the complete assignment is presented in several short segments rather than all at one time.

Advantage

More difficult or complex tasks may become more manageable if not presented all at once. Short versions of longer assignments may appear less threatening or overwhelming to the student.

Example

Provide the student with three assignments of 10 math problems each, rather than 30 problems at one time, or have the student complete only 15 to 20 of the total amount.

Suggested Uses

This strategy should be used to minimize behavior problems in students who have difficulty working for extended periods of time.

Inclusive Considerations

The teacher should make sure that (a) students know that they are expected to complete each shortened assignment, and (b) others in the classroom benefit from this strategy in addition to the mainstreamed learners.

Teaching Strategy: Individualized Instruction

Description

Instruction and classroom management procedures are designed and implemented so that individual needs and abilities are addressed.

Advantages

Classroom assignments and other expectations are made specific and appropriate to individual needs, interests, and abilities. Also, motivation may be increased through use of this strategy.

Example

Select stories or other reading material of specific interest to the student to ensure that individual interest needs are met.

Suggested Uses

Individualized instruction may be applied in most content areas and classroom settings. It is particularly useful when students must review or reinforce specific skills.

Inclusive Considerations

The teacher should implement individualized instruction in a way that does not place unrealistic expectations on the student or teacher and does not draw negative attention to the student. If possible, the teacher should individualize instruction for other students in the class, not just for those with special learning needs.

Teaching Strategy: Alternative Methods for Response

Description

The manner in which students provide answers or other responses to questions or issues is varied to meet individual needs.

Advantage

Students are allowed to respond to assigned tasks in ways compatible with their needs, ensuring that they receive the best possible chance to show that they have acquired and retained information.

Example

Allow students to tape-record responses or type them out using a computer or typewriter when they experience difficulties with writing.

Suggested Uses

Many different independent or one-to-one assignments or tasks may be responded to in alternative ways. These include reading, problem solving, math, and writing activities and assignments.

Inclusive Considerations

The teacher should make sure that students know that alternative responses are acceptable and encouraged and that they are familiar with how to apply alternative methods for responding in different activities.

Teaching Strategy: Learning Centers

Description

Specific areas are designated within the classroom where materials and activities are available for independent individual or group use.

Advantage

Students may reinforce specific skills at a pace commensurate with their own individual abilities.

Example

Create areas within the classroom where students may read along with a tape-recorded book, work cooperatively on math problems, or play learning games that reinforce needed skills.

Suggested Uses

This strategy is appropriate for reinforcing or developing many academic skills. It also is useful for developing independent work habits and allows students the opportunity to complete assigned tasks while the teacher is engaged in other activities with other students in the class.

Inclusive Considerations

The teacher should make sure that students know and understand the rules for using the learning centers and should provide peer assistance, when necessary, to facilitate student use of the centers.

Teaching Strategy: Modifying Presentations of Abstract Concepts

Description

Presentation of abstract concepts is supplemented with concrete examples, visuals, or activities; progress toward the abstractions is made gradually and systematically.

Advantage

This strategy allows students who have difficulty grasping a concept to better understand an idea while continuing to work on material that others in the class are completing.

Example

Supplement the verbal discussion of the concept of distance with visuals or manipulatives, gradually withdrawing the hands-on experiences as necessary. Provide these concrete experiences during the discussion to those who have difficulty grasping the concept in the abstract.

Suggested Uses

This strategy is appropriate for use in many content areas or situations in the classroom. Many students with learning problems can be taught material similar to that of their peers if this strategy is used on a regular basis.

Inclusive Considerations

The inability to understand more complex presentations may confront many mainstreamed students. The teacher can greatly facilitate learning complex issues or tasks in mainstream classes through regular use of concrete examples to supplement abstract presentations.

Teaching Strategy: Simplifying Reading Level of Material

Description

The complexity level of vocabulary or concepts in written material is reduced to allow students to complete various reading tasks.

Advantage

Through use of this strategy, learners may read material similar to others in the class without requiring an excessive amount of individual attention from the teacher.

Example

Place a transparency over a page of written material and, with a fine-point marker, cross out the more difficult words and write simpler equivalents of those words above or in the margin next to the crossed-out words. As the student reads, he or she substitutes the simpler words for those marked out.

Suggested Uses

This strategy should be used with students who are at lower reading levels than their peers but who also could benefit from the material in question. It will work best with students who function slightly below the reading level of the material.

Inclusive Considerations

Mainstreamed students who are slightly below the reading level of the material in any subject area are the best candidates for this strategy, especially as it allows them to work on material others in the class are completing.

Teaching Strategy: Peer Tutoring

Description

Students help other learners of similar or different ages in the classroom to complete assignments or other responsibilities.

Advantage

Learning gains are experienced by those being tutored and by the tutor in a setting that allows the teacher to simultaneously work with others in the classroom.

Example

One student in the classroom may present vocabulary words to other students in the class who require additional work with those words. The student who is the tutor is reviewing the words while those being tutored are attempting to master the vocabulary.

Suggested Uses

This strategy may be used to help mainstreamed students to review most material or acquire selected material. It is also appropriate to assist in answering student questions or in reminding the student of class rules or procedures.

Inclusive Considerations

The teacher should allow the mainstreamed student to periodically act as tutor and should ensure that the student is aware of proper procedures associated with a peer-tutoring situation.

Teaching Strategy: Prompting

Description

Learners are provided with different cues, prompts, or clues to facilitate completion of a response or task.

Advantage

Prompting allows students to complete tasks they may otherwise fail to complete and increases the probability of providing correct responses.

Example

Help the student to focus on the similarities and differences between similar words by underlining the identical or different word elements. The underlining "prompt" will assist the student in focusing on the similarities or differences.

Suggested Uses

Verbal and nonverbal prompts should be used to reduce failure on the part of the student in any subject area, especially if one or two prompts help the learner to successfully complete the task.

Inclusive Considerations

The teacher should provide prompts to mainstreamed and other learners so that the mainstreamed student does not feel singled out. The teacher should also reduce prompts gradually once they are introduced to ensure success and transition to more independent learning.

Teaching Strategy: Signal Interference

Description

Nonverbal cues are used to signal students to stop engaging in a particular activity or behavior.

Advantage

This strategy prevents minor behavior problems from escalating into bigger problems while not drawing obvious attention to the student(s) involved in the behaviors.

Example

Turn the classroom lights on and off to signal to the class that the noise level is too high and that it must be reduced.

Suggested Uses

Signal interference may be used with individuals or groups and is most useful in minimizing minor inappropriate behaviors. This is particularly effective during transition times and independent seatwork time in the classroom.

Inclusive Considerations

The teacher should strategically employ signal interference on a regular basis with mainstreamed students so they become familiar with the strategy.

Teaching Strategy: Proximity Control

Description

Strategic positioning of the teacher or student within the classroom is used to encourage appropriate behavior and minimize the possibility of inappropriate behaviors.

Advantage

Through prevention of inappropriate behaviors due to the proximity of the teacher or other students, time on task and assignment completion may be increased.

Example

Seating a student away from the area in which small-group work occurs may serve to minimize distractions experienced by the learner.

Suggested Uses

Different subject areas or educational tasks will produce various activity levels in students. Allowing the student to work in different places may increase work production or minimize anxiety associated with any subject area.

Inclusive Considerations

The teacher should use teacher or student proximity control in ways in which the student remains part of the overall classroom activities and group. Efforts should be made to minimize the "singling-out" effects often associated with this strategy.

Teaching Strategy: Touch Control

Description

Touch is used to control or minimize minor inappropriate behaviors without drawing much attention to the student.

Advantage

Touch control allows the teacher to quietly and quickly get a learner back on task or under control with little or no interruption of class activities.

Example

Walk up to the student and gently tap him or her on the shoulder as a signal to get back to the task at hand.

Suggested Uses

This strategy is most appropriate for use with younger students and may be used to reduce many minor seatwork off-task behaviors, especially during independent worktime.

Inclusive Considerations

The teacher should exercise caution when using this strategy. Some students dislike even simple tap-on-the-shoulder-type touching, and its use should be avoided with these learners. Also, this strategy may not be appropriate for older students.

Teaching Strategy: Planned Ignoring

Description

Behavior is purposely and consistently ignored in a preplanned manner to reduce the occurrence of the behavior.

Advantage

Use of this strategy eliminates unnecessary attention drawn to minor misbehavior, which shows the student that teacher attention for the misbehavior will not occur.

Example

The teacher plans in advance to ignore some off-task behavior typically exhibited by the student at the same time each day during independent worktime.

Suggested Uses

This strategy is appropriate for use with students to reduce behavior problems or off-task behaviors if the learner brings himself or herself back to task without needing direct teacher intervention.

Inclusive Considerations

The teacher should make sure that the mainstreamed students are not requesting necessary assistance through their actions. Ignoring should increase appropriate behavior and work production, especially during independent worktime or less teacher-directed activities.

Teaching Strategy: Clear and Concise Expectations

Description

Learners are provided with specific academic and behavioral expectations, ensuring that they are familiar with those expectations.

Advantage

Unclear expectations are minimized through this strategy, and frustration due to ambiguity in the classroom is reduced.

Example

After identifying specific acceptable classroom behaviors, state these clearly and concisely so that each student understands what is meant by acceptable behavior.

Suggested Uses

This strategy should be followed on a regular basis in the classroom and applied to all kinds of situations (e.g., independent worktime, large-group discussion, small-group time).

Inclusive Considerations

Some mainstreamed students may require a more specific breakdown of general class rules and procedures than others in the class in order to best understand and follow the routines. The teacher should provide these as necessary for any learner in the class.

Teaching Strategy: Time-Out

Description

The student is removed from his or her workstation because of inappropriate behavior in order to reduce external stimuli.

Advantage

This strategy offers the student an opportunity to regain control over him- or herself while thinking about the situation that preceded the time-out in order to prevent future problems.

Example

Remove the student to a quiet area in the classroom when he or she is unable to respond to a situation in a nonaggressive manner, returning him or her to the situation after a brief cooling-down period has elapsed.

Suggested Uses

Time-out can be very effective in preventing minor behaviors from escalating or in reducing the effects of a major problem. It should be used sparingly and individually, as it will not always generate desired results for different students.

Inclusive Considerations

The teacher should make sure that time-out is not overused with mainstreamed students and that it is used in ways that do not create additional problems for the student because he or she may feel "singled out." The teacher should try to ensure that students accurately interpret his or her use of time-out.

Teaching Strategy: Planned Physical Movement

Description

Students are allowed the opportunity to move about the classroom for appropriate reasons to rotate periodically from passive to active tasks.

Advantage

Periodic movement allows students to constructively release stored energy as a result of less active activities. This may help to prevent or minimize behavior problems.

Example

Allow students to go to different workstations in order to complete a series of assigned tasks.

Suggested Uses

Planned movement should be built into a student's schedule after passive, quiet activities occur. This includes working at different places in the room, running errands, or simply stretching after sitting for extended periods of time.

Inclusive Considerations

Some mainstreamed students may require regular and more frequent opportunities to move about the room. The teacher should allow this as long as movement is for a planned and constructive purpose.

Teaching Strategy: Student Accountability

Description

Students are held accountable and responsible for their own actions through various types of rewards or consequences.

Advantage

Students learn responsibility as they become aware of the connection between their actions and what follows those actions.

Example

Any consistent implementation of planned rewards or consequences will assist with student accountability for actions taken.

Suggested Uses

This strategy should prevail throughout the student's program as rewards or consequences are established and maintained for completion of work or for behaviors exhibited in the classroom.

Inclusive Considerations

Mainstreamed learners must see the connection between their actions and classroom rewards or consequences. Teachers should ensure that students are aware of the connection to avoid failure and increase student accountability in academics and behaviors.

Student Learning Strategies

Specific classroom-level efforts to address the various learning styles of students (see Chapter 2) within the context of curriculum adaptation may be effectively implemented through use of one or more learning strategy clusters. The primary purpose of learning strategies is to increase control over the use of strategies that increase the capacity for learning

(Collier & Hoover, 1987). Effectively meeting individual needs necessitates student acquisition, mastery, and generalization of the use of learning strategies.

This section presents six learning strategies that enhance student learning within content areas. The format used to present the strategies is similar to that used in the previous section. It includes a general description, identification of the learning styles (as discussed in Chapter 1) that are most affected by its use, major elements, classroom uses, general education classroom considerations, and a detailed example of how each strategy may be taught to students. The teacher and student items in these examples reflect statements or questions of a general nature. They may be applied to specific situations as different occasions arise. The examples illustrate how a teacher may help a student to learn the procedures associated with each strategy. As the student becomes more proficient in the use of learning strategies, individual needs may be met and potential problems with curriculum implementation may be minimized. Table 3.1 provides an overview of the six learning strategies and selected curricular areas that are affected by their use in the classroom.

Learning Strategy: Active Processing

Description

The use of questions generated by the student relative to the particular subject in efforts to activate prior knowledge or assist in elaborating upon that subject area.

Style Development

Active processing assists in the development of tempo, persistence, and locus of control.

Elements

Self-talk, self-questioning, and self-reinforcement are important elements. This strategy also emphasizes scanning, summarizing, generating questions, predicting, and elaborating upon information to be learned through self-talk and self-questioning.

Classroom Uses

Active processing is appropriate for assisting in language development, becoming aware of the learning process, and reflective tempo development; reducing low-persistence behaviors; or reducing confusion in locus of control.

Table 3.1
Cognitive Learning Strategies and Curriculum Adaptation

Strategy	Key Elements	Curriculum Areas
Active processing	Self-talk Self-question Self-reinforce	Increase language development Access prior knowledge Develop awareness of learning process Develop reflective tempo Reduce low-persistence behaviors Reduce confusion in locus of control
Analogy	Rhyme Schema Metaphor	Develop higher tolerance for new/unusual Access prior knowledge Develop categorization skills
Coping	Confront Engage Solve Ask for aid Implement Persist Outcome/solution	Encourage problem solving Develop higher tolerance for new/unusual Build self-esteem Develop higher-persistence skills Lower anxiety levels Reduce confusion in locus of control
Evaluation	Self-monitor Check Reflect Transfer	Increase awareness of learning process Develop field-sensitive skills Develop/utilize field-independent skills Develop reflective tempo Develop categorization skills Develop higher-persistence strategies Lower anxiety level Reduce confusion in locus of control
Organization	Group Cluster Label	Develop association skills Develop analytical skills Increase cognitive development Develop field-independent skills Develop field-sensitive skills Develop categorization skills
Rehearsal	Review Recite Recall	Increase language development Improve retention of information Develop higher tolerance for new/unusual Develop reflective tempo

Note. From *Cognitive Learning Styles for Minority Handicapped Students*, by C. Collier and J. J. Hoover, 1987, Boulder, CO: Hamilton Publications.

Inclusive Considerations

Students must be made aware that self-talk strategies are appropriate and acceptable. Teachers should demonstrate how and in what manner self-talk may be used by the student in the classroom, helping him or her to define, specify, evaluate, monitor, and complete an assignment or task.

Example

Step 1: Definition

TEACHER: "First, you need to think about what you intend to accomplish in this task. What is it you plan to do? What is your goal?"

STUDENT: "First, I need to make sure that I know what I am going to do."

Step 2: Specification

TEACHER: "Second, you need to decide what you will need to do to accomplish the task or goal."

STUDENT: "Next, I need to decide what to do to reach my goal."

Step 3: Evaluation

TEACHER: "Third, you must check what you have done. Has your action provided the correct answer?"

STUDENT: "I must check my work. Is there anything wrong with my answer or method?"

Step 4: Monitoring

TEACHER: "There are usually several ways to accomplish a goal. Also, remember that it is okay to make mistakes, as we can learn from our mistakes. Be sure to try another approach if the one you have tried does not appear to work."

STUDENT: "I know that more than one way usually exists to achieve a goal. I also know that mistakes can help me to learn. I will try another approach if the one I use first does not work."

Step 5: Completion

TEACHER: "Finally, you need to recognize when you have completed the task or achieved your goal. Remember what you set out to do and congratulate yourself when you have completed it."

STUDENT: "Did I complete my task? Did I do what I set out to do? When the task has been completed, I will congratulate myself for a job well done."

Learning Strategy: Analogy

Description

Analogy allows learners to recall previously experienced patterns or experiences that are similar to new items or experiences.

Style Development

Analogy assists in the development of tolerance and categorization styles of learning.

Elements

Analogy includes the use of rhyme, schema, metaphor, or clone procedures to enhance acquisition and retention of new material.

Classroom Uses

Analogy strategies are appropriate for assisting students to develop (a) higher tolerance for new or unusual situations or information, and (b) various categorization skills related to new and existing knowledge.

Inclusive Considerations

It is essential that analogies made by the teacher or students be related to students' experiences and knowledge levels. To facilitate the development of this learning strategy, teachers should assist students in recalling prior knowledge and compare, substitute, or elaborate upon that knowledge relative to new information.

Example

Step 1: Prior Knowledge

TEACHER: "Can you recall something from your own experiences that is similar to this item?"

STUDENT: "What do I know that is like this item?"

Step 2: Comparison

TEACHER: "Now examine how these items are similar or different. Do they have similar uses?"

STUDENT: "How are these items similar or different? Are they used in similar ways?"

Step 3: Substitution

TEACHER: "Identify the items or parts of items that might be substituted for these items. Why would this substitution work or not work?"

STUDENT: "Can I use these similar elements interchangeably? What other items might be substituted for these items?"

Step 4: Elaboration

TEACHER: "Think about other experiences, words, or actions in your life. In what ways are they similar to or different from this new situation?"

STUDENT: "When asked for examples, I can provide them based upon my own experiences."

Learning Strategy: Coping

Description

Coping is a problem-solving strategy that helps students to confront and solve problems and issues in an objective manner.

Style Development

The use of coping strategies assists in the development of tolerance, persistence, anxiety, and locus-of-control styles of learning.

Elements

Coping includes the use of different elements necessary to confront issues. Specifically, it includes helping learners to confront, develop solutions, obtain necessary assistance, attempt to solve the problem by implementing solutions, and continue until an acceptable solution is found.

Classroom Uses

Coping strategies are appropriate for most problem-solving situations and assist in developing greater awareness of the learning process, higher tolerance, self-esteem, and persistence skills, and in reducing confusion in locus of control.

Inclusive Considerations

Students in inclusive settings must be taught various coping strategies and may initially require that this be completed on an individual basis. The teacher should develop problem-solving skills within the context of and with sensitivity to the student's developed values. This will prove beneficial as the strategy is acquired and maintained.

Example

Step 1: Confrontation

TEACHER: "What are the essential elements of the problem? Have you controlled your feelings about the problem or its consequences?"

STUDENT: "Can I break the problem into several parts? What can I say about this problem? Have I controlled my feelings relative to the problem?"

Step 2: Plan Strategy

TEACHER: "Break the problem into parts and list them in the order in which they should be addressed. Develop a plan for addressing the problem in a step-by-step manner. Imagine what the solution or answer might be. How will you know that you have resolved the problem?"

STUDENT: "What are the elements of this problem that must be addressed? In what order should I address the elements? What might possible solutions look like? How will I know that I have resolved the problem?"

Step 3: Assistance

TEACHER: "Study the elements of the problem. Do you need help with any of them? Where might you go to find necessary help? Everyone needs help from time to time. You must recognize when you need help and know how to go about finding it."

STUDENT: "Do I need help with any parts of this problem? I know that it is okay to ask for help. Do I know someone who can help me? Do I know how to get the necessary help?"

Step 4: Implementation

TEACHER: "After you have analyzed your problem and come up with a plan for taking action, you must use that plan. Knowing that you are starting your plan is important in coping with problems and situations. You may use a gesture or word to signal that you have begun your plan."

STUDENT: "When I am ready to begin addressing my problem, I will snap my fingers or nod my head. I will know that I am ready to begin when I have my action plan ready and have identified possible sources of help."

Step 5: Persistence

TEACHER: "There are usually several ways to achieve something or solve a problem. Some ways may be more effective than others in different circumstances. Do not stop trying if you have difficulty or meet resistance to solving the problem. Sometimes you must try another approach to achieve a solution. Think of other times when you had difficulty reaching a solution and what you did to resolve that problem."

STUDENT: "I will not stop if I meet with difficulty or resistance. I will attempt different solutions to the problem until the problem has been resolved."

Step 6: Resolution

TEACHER: "Part of coping with problems is to recognize that a solution has been reached and that the problem has been resolved. Recall what it was you were attempting to accomplish and what you imagined the solution to be like. When you reach this accomplishment and have a solution that addresses the problem, then you can say to yourself that you have resolved this problem. Congratulate yourself for coping with and solving your own problems."

STUDENT: "I have addressed my problem, developed and implemented a plan of action, modified the plan as necessary, asked for necessary help, and generated an appropriate solution. I was able to resolve my problem because I am able to ask for help when I need it. The solution that I have reached solves my problem. I congratulate myself for solving my own problems."

Learning Strategy: Evaluation

Description

Evaluation is a strategy that assists in the development of awareness of what is necessary to complete tasks or monitor behavior related to various educational situations.

Style Development

Field, tempo, categorization, persistence, anxiety, and locus-of-control styles of learning are addressed through use of the evaluation learning strategy.

Elements

Evaluation includes the appropriate use of self-monitoring, reflection, prediction, and transfer skills as students attempt to study and evaluate situations and tasks.

Classroom Uses

This strategy has many appropriate classroom uses, including developing field-sensitivity, reflective tempo, higher persistence, and lower anxiety abilities, as well as reducing confusion in locus of control.

Inclusive Considerations

The independent work habits of students who are in general education classrooms may be improved significantly as evaluation abilities are acquired and used in the classroom. Demonstration of the proper ways to check answers, monitor behavior, reflect upon results, and transfer skills to new situations will prove beneficial to mainstreamed students in their development of this learning strategy.

Example

Step 1: Analysis

TEACHER: "You must analyze the task to determine what it requires. This includes items such as materials, time, space, or types of actions. What is the expected outcome of the task? What steps must you follow in order to complete the task? Review other completed assignments to determine possible steps you might take to complete this task."

STUDENT: "What do I need to do to complete this task, and do I have all necessary materials and resources? What should the expected outcome look like? What steps must I follow to effectively achieve the expected outcome?"

Step 2: Strategy Identification

TEACHER: "After you have analyzed the task, you must identify possible strategies that might be used to complete the task. Think about strategies you have used in the past to complete similar tasks. One or more of these may be necessary to finish this task."

STUDENT: "What strategies do I know that might be useful for this particular task? Why might these be useful in this particular situation?"

Step 3: Strategy Implementation

TEACHER: "Prior to using a selected strategy, review the steps in that strategy. Remember that one strategy may be used in several different situations and that different situations may require the use of more than one strategy."

STUDENT: "I have selected these strategies for this task. I will review the process associated with each strategy prior to using it. I will use these strategies while I complete this task."

Step 4: Feedback

TEACHER: "You must become aware of how helpful it is to use the strategies you have selected. They assist you to complete the task correctly and efficiently. Stop at times to think about how you are doing and how effective the strategies are for completing the task at hand."

STUDENT: "How useful is this strategy for this particular task? Is this strategy helping me to correctly and efficiently do the assigned task? Do I need to use a different strategy?"

Step 5: Elaboration and Generalization

TEACHER: "Think of other previously completed tasks where use of one or more of these strategies would have been helpful in doing the tasks. Could you have completed those tasks more efficiently had you used these strategies? Think of other types of tasks or future tasks where you might appropriately use one or more of these strategies."

STUDENT: "Why were these strategies useful to this particular task? In what other types of situations would the use of these strategies be helpful?"

Learning Strategy: Organization

Description

The strategy of organization pertains to student abilities to group or cluster items in various and appropriate ways relative to specific tasks.

Style Development

The styles of learning related to field and categorization are developed through specific uses of this learning strategy.

Elements

The organization strategy includes the elements of grouping, clustering, sorting, labeling, and studying items to facilitate effective use of groupings in a learning situation or task.

Classroom Uses

Classroom uses of the organization strategy include development of association skills, field-independent and field-sensitive abilities, and the ability to categorize items for meaningful use in learning.

Inclusive Considerations

Some students placed in inclusive education settings may experience difficulties with knowing what types of categorization or cluster groupings are appropriate in different situations. The teacher should directly teach possible ways in which items may be grouped and used in learning situations, which will help these students best understand different concepts and learning tasks.

Example

Step 1: Sorting

TEACHER: "Items can be organized in various ways, depending upon their function and use. Think about how things in your home or room are organized and what might occur if some pattern for sorting and organizing items did not exist."

STUDENT: "I must examine these items and identify similar elements or patterns within them. I am searching for ways to sort and organize the items into meaningful clusters with shared characteristics."

Step 2: Labeling

TEACHER: "To assist you in remembering the individual items in your pattern or cluster, it helps to give a label to the whole group, based upon shared characteristics."

STUDENT: "Based upon the patterns that I perceive, I will provide a name for each of the groups of items I am trying to learn."

Step 3: Studying

TEACHER: "Examine the items individually and in their groups. Study the whole group and individual items together. This will enable you to more easily remember the group and individual items because you have linked them together."

STUDENT: "I will practice grouping these items. I will examine the individual items in their groups to better remember each item and associated group."

Step 4: Self-Test

TEACHER: "While looking at the items, say the names of the groups to yourself. Then, without looking at the items, say the names of the groups and the individual items within the groups. Practice this several times until you recall each group name and associated individual items without looking at the items. This will help you to organize what you are learning and to check to see whether or not your organization is effective in helping you to learn the items and associated groups."

STUDENT: "I will review the groups and associated items by saying them without looking at the individual items. I will check to see that my organization of the items is helping me to remember the items and groups by saying the names of the groups without looking at the items."

Learning Strategy: Rehearsal

Description

Rehearsal emphasizes the practice of teaching students to think about what they are doing (a) prior to beginning a task, or (b) periodically during a task to increase comprehension and retention.

Style Development

Tolerance and tempo learning-style abilities are emphasized through use of the rehearsal strategy.

Elements

The elements of review, recite, and recall related to different aspects associated with a learning task or situation are important in the rehearsal strategy.

Classroom Uses

The classroom uses of this strategy include helping students to develop (a) a greater tolerance for new situations, (b) reflective tempo, and (c) a greater awareness for using familiar items or skills in unknown situations.

Inclusive Considerations

The teacher must teach the specific process associated with implementing a rehearsal strategy to students in general education classrooms and provide opportunities to practice how to rehearse both during a task and prior to beginning the task. A primary goal for rehearsing is to think through what one is doing, which may minimize problems and increase effective use of time.

Example

Step 1: Pause

TEACHER: "Learn to stop after each new idea, passage, or element and review it in your mind."

STUDENT: "What have I just heard, read, or seen? I will mentally review these as I am learning them."

Step 2: Question

TEACHER: "After reviewing the idea, ask questions that will help you to remember the topic."

STUDENT: "I will ask myself questions about what I have just read, heard, or seen in order to best remember the information."

Step 3: Visualize

TEACHER: "When you stop to review what has just occurred, make a mental picture of the idea."

STUDENT: "I will create a mental picture or movie depicting what has just occurred."

Step 4: Summarize

TEACHER: "When you have finished reading or listening, summarize to yourself what has occurred. Now when you need to remember this information, you need to only recall the summary."

STUDENT: "I will organize my questions, responses, and visualizations. I will attempt to remember the most important points and form a summary picture to help me remember the information."

Student Study Strategies

Study strategies are tactics designed to assist in the completion of various tasks in a variety of content and skill areas. Twenty-three study strategies are presented in Table 3.2. The purpose of presenting these strategies is to familiarize teachers with useful task-related practices. The table, which was developed by Hoover and Patton (1995), provides overview information regarding each selected strategy, including (a) emphasized task area in which the strategy can be used, (b) the general process associated with the strategy, and (c) comments related to classroom use. The table includes the more frequently discussed study strategies, but it is not all-inclusive. Furthermore, not all strategies are appropriate for use in all inclusive or special class settings. They do represent additional strategies that may be effective as curriculum adaptations are needed.

Use of these strategies by students may facilitate better task completion and retention of information while simultaneously helping them to

Table 3.2
Student Study Strategies

Strategy	Task Areas	Process	Classroom Applications
CAN-DO	Acquiring content	Create list of items to learn Ask self if list is complete Note details and main ideas Describe components and their relationships Overlearn main items followed by learning details	This strategy may assist with memorization of lists of items through rehearsal techniques.
COPS	Written reports	Capitalization correct Overall appearance Punctuation correct Spelling correct	This strategy provides a structure for proofreading written work prior to submitting it to the teacher.
DEFENDS	Written expression	Decide on a specific position Examine own reasons for this position Form list of points explaining each reason Expose position in first sentence of written task Note each reason and associated points Drive home position in last sentence Search for and correct any errors	This strategy assists learners to defend a particular position in a written assignment.
EASY	Study content	Elicit questions (who, what, where, when, why) Ask self which information is least difficult	EASY may assist learners to organize and prioritize information by responding to questions designed to identify important content to be learned.

(Continues)

Table 3.2 *Continued*

Strategy	Task Areas	Process	Classroom Applications
FIST	Reading comprehension	Study easy content initially, followed by difficult content Yes—provide self-reinforcement First sentence is read Indicate a question based on material in first sentence Search for answer to question Tie question and answer together through paraphrasing	This questioning strategy assists students to actively pursue responses to questions related directly to material being read.
GLP	Note taking	Guided Lecture Procedure	GLP provides students with a structure for taking notes during lectures. Group activity is involved to facilitate effective note taking.
PANORAMA	Reading	Preparatory Stage—identify purpose Intermediate Stage—survey and read Concluding Stage—memorize material	This strategy includes a three-stage process to assist with reading comprehension.
PARS	Reading	Preview Ask questions Read Summarize	PARS is recommended for use with younger students and with those who have limited experiences with study strategies.
PENS	Sentence writing	Pick a formula Explore different words to fit into the formula Note the words selected Subject and verb selections follow	PENS is appropriate for developing basic sentence structure and assists students in writing different types of sentences by following formulas for sentence construction.

PIRATES	Test Taking	Prepare to succeed Inspect instructions carefully Read entire question, remember memory strategies, and reduce choices Answer question or leave until later Turn back to the abandoned items Estimate unknown answers by avoiding absolutes and eliminating similar choices Survey to ensure that all items have a response	PIRATES may assist learners to more carefully and successfully complete tests.
PQ4R	Reading	Preview Question Read Reflect Recite Review	PQ4R may assist students to become more discriminating readers.
RAP	Reading comprehension	Read paragraph Ask self to identify the main idea and two supporting details Put main idea and details into own words	This strategy assists students in learning information through paraphrasing.
RARE	Reading	Review selection questions Answer all questions known Read the selection Express answers to remaining questions	RARE emphasizes reading for a specific purpose while focusing on acquiring answers to selection questions initially not known.
RDPE	Underlining	Read entire passage Decide which ideas are important	This strategy assists learners in organizing and remembering main points and ideas

(*Continues*)

Table 3.2 *Continued*

Strategy	Task Areas	Process	Classroom Applications
		Plan the underlining to include only main points Evaluate results of the underlining by reading only the underlined words	in a reading selection through appropriate underlining of key words.
REAP	Reading Writing Thinking	Read Encode Annotate Ponder	REAP is a method that assists students in combining several skills to facilitate discussion about reading material.
ReQuest	Reading Questioning	Reciprocal Questioning	Teacher and student ask each other questions about a selection. Student modeling of teacher questions and teacher feedback are emphasized as the learner explores the meaning of the reading material.
RIDER	Reading comprehension	Read sentence Image (form mental picture) Describe how new image differs from previous sentence Evaluate image to ensure that it contains all necessary elements Repeat process with subsequent sentences	This visual imagery strategy cues the learner to form a mental image of what was previously learned from a sentence just read.
SCORER	Test taking	Schedule time effectively Clue words identified Omit difficult items until end Read carefully Estimate answers requiring calculations Review work and responses	This test-taking strategy provides a structure for completing various tests by assisting students in carefully and systematically completing test items.

SQRQCQ	Math word problems	Survey word problem Question asked is identified Read more carefully Question process required to solve problem Compute the answer Question self to ensure that the answer solves the problem	This strategy provides a systematic structure for identifying the question being asked in a math word problem, computing the response, and ensuring that the question in the problem was answered.
SQ3R	Reading	Survey Question Read Recite Review	SQ3R provides a systematic approach to improve reading comprehension.
SSCD	Vocabulary development	Sound clues used Structure clues used Context clues used Dictionary used	SSCD encourages students to remember to use sound, structure, and context clues to address unfamiliar vocabulary. This is followed by dictionary usage, if necessary.
TOWER	Written reports	Think Order ideas Write Edit Rewrite	TOWER provides a structure for completing initial and final drafts of written reports. It may be used effectively with COPS.
TQLR	Listening	Tuning in Questioning Listening Reviewing	This strategy assists with listening comprehension. Students generate questions and listen for specific statements related to those questions.

Note. From *Teaching Students with Learning Problems to Use Study Skills*, by J. J. Hoover and J. R. Patton, 1995, Austin, TX: PRO-ED. Copyright 1995 by PRO-ED, Inc. Used by permission.

become more independent learners. The reader is referred to the sources used to develop the table for additional information about and references for particular study strategies. The information provided in the table will help educators to identify various strategies for different curriculum task areas that may be used by students to meet their individual learning and behavior needs. Although each study strategy presented has its own process, educators should follow the general guidelines given at the beginning of this section to help students in acquiring and maintaining the different strategies within the overall curriculum adaptation process.

In addition, one current teaching practice that advocates the integration of learning through a variety of instructional strategies is cooperative learning. As students engage in cooperative learning, curriculum adaptation needs are met in interrelated ways. The concept of meeting students' curricular needs as addressed in this book is one of ensuring that curricular elements are emphasized in interrelated ways to obtain the best teaching and learning results. Thus, cooperative learning and its principles are highly compatible with our adaptation emphasis. The use of cooperative learning is left to the discretion of teachers, based upon individual classroom situations. However, should cooperative learning be used in meeting the curriculum adaptation needs of students, the teacher will find its practices highly compatible with addressing the interrelated elements of content, instructional strategies, instructional settings, and student behaviors. The following discussion provides an overview of cooperative learning, along with ideas as to how this method may be used in curriculum adaptation for students with learning and behavior problems.

Cooperative Learning

Several researchers have written extensively on the topic of cooperative learning (Johnson & Johnson, 1990; Kagan, 1990; Slavin, 1991). According to Johnson and Johnson (1990), cooperative learning "is the instructional use of small groups so that students work together to maximize their own and one another's learning" (p. 69). This contrasts with competitive and highly individualistic learning. Although competition and individualistic learning can be part of cooperative learning, they are achieved and become effective through cooperative efforts (Johnson & Johnson, 1987). Cooperative learning teams may be composed of a small group of students or a pair of students working together. In some situations (e.g., general education) where many students with learning problems are educated, the use of pairs may represent the best initial structure. Whether in pairs or in small groups, the principles of cooperative learning may easily be incorporated into the classroom.

Essential Elements

Although the different researchers in this area have identified different variations in ways of implementing cooperative learning, several common elements are frequently discussed. These include, as identified by Roy (1990):

- positive interdependence
- individual accountability
- opportunities for interactions
- interpersonal training
- group processing

Within the context of cooperative learning, students perceive that their goals are achieved through shared work with their peers. The five elements just identified facilitate this shared work in curriculum adaptation in any content area. Each of these components is briefly summarized below (Johnson & Johnson, 1990; Roy, 1990).

Positive interdependence occurs when each student in the cooperative group or pair feels a sense of mutual goals and rewards. Each student understands that all members must complete the assigned tasks for the group's work to be complete. Students learn the material or task themselves and assist others in acquiring the information.

Individual accountability reflects the commitment to ensuring that each member demonstrates mastery of the assigned task, skill, or content. Assessment of each student's mastery levels, as well as of those of the cooperative learning team, occurs. Cooperative learning does not exclude or excuse individuals from participating or from acquiring the material. Rather, it is a structure designed to use the strengths of each group member to facilitate the learning of the task or skill.

Opportunities for interactions means that students are encouraged to assist others in learning material. This includes exchanging ideas, providing feedback, encouraging student efforts, discussing concepts and skills, and supporting one another's involvement. This positive and constructive interaction not only helps those being provided assistance, but also offers a valuable learning experience for those doing the helping. Although the quantity and quality of these types of student interactions will vary, regular practice in facilitating student assistance and interactions strengthens the sharing of information in a cooperative manner.

Interpersonal training addresses the issue of preparing students for successful interactions in cooperative learning teams. Teachers must assist students with communication, conflict-management, decision making, leadership, and other related group-oriented interaction skills. Students with special learning needs may require assistance and encouragement in this area. The use of pairs or groups of three students, some of whom possess these skills, allows students the opportunity to share their skills with others. The success of cooperative pairs or groups relies heavily upon proper student preparation by the teacher in how the teams should function. In many situations, the direct teaching of specific study skills will facilitate this student preparation (e.g., self-management of behavior, note taking/outlining, time management).

Group processing gives students and teachers the opportunity to determine how well the pair or group functioned relative to specific tasks. Cooperative team members discuss individual contributions to the group, ways to improve overall member interactions and contributions, and recommendations for future cooperative team efforts. Use of a student or teacher observer of the group's activities may facilitate the processing of the group's interactions.

Implementation

A cooperative learning environment in the classroom requires emphasis on each of the five elements. Once teachers have ensured that students possess a minimum level of skills necessary for group interaction (i.e., interpersonal training), cooperative learning may begin. The structure of activities, lessons, room arrangements, and evaluation of performance will vary across cooperative learning groups. Research in the area of cooperative learning provides evidence of its effectiveness with students. According to Slavin (1991), cooperative learning is effective in enhancing student achievement in all major "subject areas in elementary and secondary grades, and for low, average, and high achieving students." Slavin stated further that "cooperative learning usually supplements the teacher's interaction by giving students an opportunity to discuss information or practice skills originally presented by the teacher" (p. 83).

In support, Johnson and Johnson (1990) wrote that cooperative learning is effective in helping students to learn basic facts, understand concepts, problem solve, and use higher-level thinking skills. The learning components discussed in the previous section that are addressed through study-skill use represent higher-level thinking skills as well as problem solving and concept development (i.e., acquisition, recording, organization, memorization, synthesis, and location). Of the five critical elements associated with cooperative learning, Slavin (1991) found that individual accountability and group processing were the most important to the success of this approach.

Curriculum Adaptation and Cooperative Learning

In reference to the education of students with special learning needs, Johnson and Johnson (1986) found cooperative learning strategies to be effective with students with disabilities. Salend (1994) cited several researchers who supported the use of cooperative learning for students with learning problems who are placed in inclusive settings.

When implementing cooperative learning, the teacher should follow several guidelines. These were developed from information found in several sources and summarize factors important to the success of cooperative learning (Johnson & Johnson, 1990):

- The group or pair produces one product.
- Team members assist others.
- Team members seek assistance when necessary from other team members.
- Team members discuss ideas prior to changing any previously agreed upon ideas or issues.
- Each team member accepts responsibility for the completed project or task.
- Each member participates in the group activities.
- Each member provides input into the group processing aspect of the team's activities.
- Individual accountability for learning the task or concept prevails, along with expectations of group interactions.

Cooperative learning has been found to be effective in various subject areas with a variety of students who possess varying skill levels. It is a teaching practice that facilitates effective implementation and adaptation of curricula in special and inclusive class settings. The implementation of cooperative learning may involve a variety of groupings or pairs with an emphasis on different content areas or behavior skills. For purposes of these discussions, the reader is advised to consider curriculum adaptations within the structure of cooperative learning. For more detailed discussions about specific strategies for implementing cooperative learning, the reader is referred to Johnson, Johnson, Holubec, and Roy (1984) and Kagan (1990).

Technology and Curriculum Adaptation

Current technological advances provide wonderful opportunities for meeting curriculum adaptation needs of students with learning and behavioral problems. Use of computers, electronic communications, or distance learning offers students greater access to information and learning, which in turn facilitates greater success in school. The increased availability of computers in teaching and learning provides unique opportunities for both educators and students as curriculum adaptations are determined and implemented.

For example, Hofmeister et al. (1994) discussed computer-based expert technology that helps educators identify appropriate assessment devices and intervention strategies for addressing specific learning and behavior problems. One particular program, The SMH.PAL System (Hofmeister et al., 1994), provides immediate and relevant descriptions of numerous forms of interventions for problems such as aggression, impulsivity, lack of social interaction skills, or immature behavior. This program gives the user suggested articles describing research and appropriate intervention strategies for the specified problem. Thus, this type of technology offers educators current information to meet one or more identified curriculum adaptation needs.

Another technology application used to assess student social skills was described by Irvin and Walker (1994). In this program, video presentations of social events and computer-based student responses are employed. Results may be used to develop or adapt curricula to meet specific behavioral needs. Still another program, Ecobehavioral Assessment Systems Software (EBASS) was described by Greenwood, Carta, Kamps, Terry, and Delquadri (1994). EBASS is a computer-based program for observing, assessing, and modifying classroom instruction. In general (and special) education services, it is necessary to conduct assessment to account for differences in student curricular needs, teacher strategies, and overall educational settings, and EBASS assists educators in these areas.

Other recent technological programs that relate to curriculum adaptation for students with learning and behavior problems are the Self-Help Interpersonal Skills (SHIP) program (Loeding & Crittenden, 1994) and Dynamath (Gerber, Semmel, & Semmel, 1994). Both have the potential to assist educators in their assessments of curriculum adaptation needs, in the selection of appropriate instructional strategies and settings relative to specific content, and in modification of inappropriate student behaviors.

Some of the potential positive effects of technology use in the classroom with students who have learning and behavior problems include increased motivation, improved self-concept, the use of alternatives to traditional teaching methods, and increased written language abilities. In a recent project, for example, Keyes (1994) found that using computers with students who have learning and behavior problems assisted in increasing their motivation to learn, which, in turn, affected self-concept, active learning, and self-analysis of progress.

Whether used to assess curriculum adaptation needs, select teaching or student strategies, provide greater access to current information (i.e., the Internet), or motivate students in their learning, current and emerging technology will continue to play a critical role in the education of students in general and special education settings.

Discussion Issues

1. Discuss possible situations in which use of the teaching and behavior management techniques discussed in this chapter may facilitate adaptation of one or more of the curricular elements.

2. Outline and discuss a program for adapting one of the four curricular elements for an individual student with special learning needs.

3. Select five teaching strategies and explain how each may be successfully implemented in an inclusive class setting.

4. Select one learning strategy and explain how this strategy can be used to effectively adapt a curriculum.

5. Demonstrate how use of cooperative learning may be effective in curriculum adaptation.

Collaboration and Curriculum Adaptation

4

. . . .

Cooperation and collaboration among special and general educators must occur to ensure success for students with special learning needs. The previous chapters of this book were devoted to one important aspect of addressing the needs of special learners (i.e., selecting and implementing specific curriculum adaptations).

Program collaboration involves the continuous exchange of knowledge, skills, and expertise between special and general educators. Specifically, topics discussed in the previous chapters must be considered by all professionals involved in ensuring an appropriate education for each student. Many teachers in general education classrooms are willing to address individual needs of learners when they feel competent about their own skills and abilities. If inclusion is to be successful, then special educators must provide support and assistance to general educators regarding curriculum adaptations for students who move from the special education classroom to the general classroom.

Relationship of Collaboration to the Curriculum Adaptation Model

One process that may be followed by special and general educators to ensure effective program collaboration in curriculum adaptation is illustrated in Figure 4.1. The process associated with this model reflects the primary goal of ensuring consistent implementation of curriculum adaptations across class settings. This model of program collaboration is characterized by three stages: development, implementation, and evaluation.

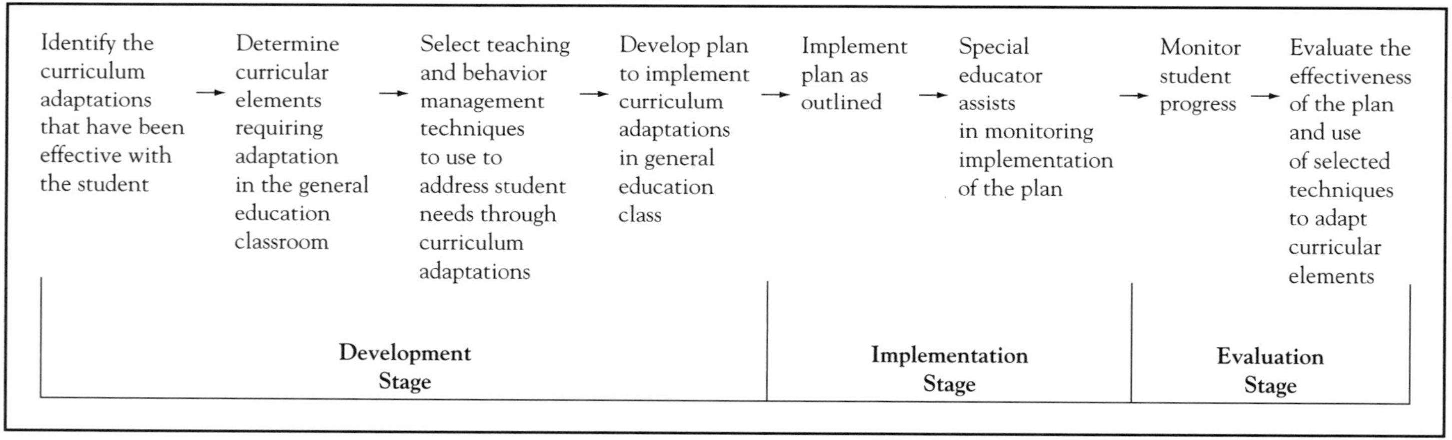

Development Stage

Identify the curriculum adaptations that have been effective with the student → Determine curricular elements requiring adaptation in the general education classroom → Select teaching and behavior management techniques to use to address student needs through curriculum adaptations → Develop plan to implement curriculum adaptations in general education class →

Implementation Stage

Implement plan as outlined → Special educator assists in monitoring implementation of the plan →

Evaluation Stage

Monitor student progress → Evaluate the effectiveness of the plan and use of selected techniques to adapt curricular elements

Figure 4.1. Model for program collaboration in curriculum adaptation. *Note.* Adapted from *Cognitive Learning Strategies for Minority Handicapped Students* (pp. 58–59), by C. Collier and J. J. Hoover, 1987, Boulder, CO: Hamilton Publications. Copyright 1987 by Hamilton Publications. Adapted with permission.

Development Stage

Curriculum adaptations employed frequently and regularly in a special education classroom can also be implemented effectively in other classes. During the development stage, the special educator must identify specific curriculum adaptations used in the special education classroom. Once identified, the curriculum followed outside special education settings is analyzed to identify specific content, instructional strategies and settings, and management procedures (i.e., the areas that require curriculum adaptation must be identified and a program developed to implement those adaptations).

Through various assessment procedures and instruments, including the *Guide for Curricular Adaptations* (discussed in Chapter 2), in which curricular elements that require adaptations are determined, teachers select appropriate teaching and behavior management techniques. The techniques used successfully for adapting curriculum in the special education classroom should be attempted initially for adapting similar curricular elements in the general education class because the student will have experienced success with use of the strategies.

Once the curricular elements that require adaptations and appropriate teaching and behavior management techniques have been selected, teachers should complete a plan for implementing the adaptations in the general education classroom. Figure 4.2 provides a guide for documenting and outlining a program for these curriculum adaptations to ensure that they are implemented consistently in both general and special class settings. The guide also serves as a reference for program evaluation of different curricular elements. Although this guide is discussed relative to adaptations in inclusive classrooms, it may be used to document program implementation in the special education classroom as well.

The *Guide for Program Implementation of Curricular Adaptations* given in the figure has been completed for illustrative purposes. The plan outlines several important factors related to the effective implementation of curriculum adaptations. The information documented in the *Guide for Curricular Adaptations* discussed in Chapter 2 is used as a base for completing the plan for program implementation. The curricular elements that require adaptations are documented, along with a specific objective that pertains to each adaptation. The objective should reduce or eliminate problems associated with one or more of the curricular elements that need adaptation. Once the adaptations objective is outlined, teachers document specific teaching or behavior management strategies to achieve this objective. The plan also provides an opportunity to delineate how the program will be implemented, its duration, and the basis for evaluating the plan and objective.

Name: Juan   Date: 6/88

Subject: History   Grade: 5

Assignment: Record notes; Participate in Discussions

Summary of Adaptation Needs:

Instructional Strategy: Lecture does not motivate Juan or facilitate effective learning

Student Behaviors: Juan frequently looks around room and taps pencil on desk

Objective(s): Increase accuracy of recorded notes and reduce off-task behaviors

Minimum Duration of Program: Three school weeks

Specific Instructions for Implementing Plan:

Present Juan with an outline of the lecture prior to the start of the lec-

ture. Assign Juan a peer tutor to answer questions he may have about the

lecture and note taking. Use a self-monitoring checklist to record off-task

behaviors as adaptation to address tapping noises.

Evaluation Procedures and Program Monitoring:

The general education teacher will review and discuss with Juan his daily

lecture notes and, using a simple checklist, record the accuracy of the

notes for the day. The special educator will also review and discuss the

daily notes with Juan. Both teachers will review daily the self-monitoring

checklist. Evaluation of the plan will include periodic discussions about the

plan between the special and general educators.

Figure 4.2.   Guide for Program Implementation of Curricular Adaptations.

Implementation Stage

Once the plan for implementing curriculum adaptations in the inclusive classroom has been developed, the general education teacher is responsible for implementing the plan and monitoring program progress (the implementation stage). Where possible, the special educator should assist the general education teacher with program implementation by providing any supports that are necessary to achieve the adaptation objective. The special educator should also assist with program monitoring.

If curriculum adaptations are to succeed, both general and special educators must be involved in the process. However, primary responsibility for implementing curriculum adaptations in inclusive settings rests with the former. Two sets of guidelines for assisting special and general educators in the overall curriculum adaptation process are provided. The first set is from the perspective of the general education teacher, and the second from that of the special educator.

Guidelines for the General Education Teacher

1. Gather information related to one or more of the curricular elements that require adaptations.

2. Implement curriculum adaptations on a regular basis for the specified amount of time.

3. Document the effectiveness of the adaptations.

4. Teach flexibly to minimize problems that may result from changes that occur as adaptations are implemented.

5. Explore options for curriculum adaptations with other educators, especially special education personnel.

6. Adapt only specific areas that require modifications and do not attempt to change too much at one time.

7. Use different adaptation techniques to achieve appropriate education for all students.

8. Implement adaptations in a manner that ensures smooth transitions into the use of different teaching and behavior management techniques.

9. Anticipate and account for potential problems that may arise from adaptations prior to implementation.

10. When possible, use adaptations that are most compatible with existing classroom structures and routines.

These guidelines emphasize flexibility in teaching and represent a commitment to using different adaptations until all students in the class receive an appropriate education. Given the complexity of needs and issues surrounding the education of students with learning or behavioral problems, general educators may require support from special educators in this area.

Guidelines for the Special Education Teacher

1. Assist in gathering and interpreting information related to curricular elements potentially requiring adaptations.

2. Assist with the adaptations of materials if necessary (e.g., simplifying reading levels of material).

3. Collaborate with general educators concerning the appropriate selection and use of different teaching and behavior management techniques.

4. Provide suggestions and materials for simple record keeping related to effectiveness of curriculum adaptations implemented in the inclusive classroom.

5. Provide direct assistance, when possible and appropriate, to general educators as adaptations are implemented.

6. Support general educators' efforts to adapt curricular elements.

7. Provide recommendations, when possible, within the existing structure in the general education classroom to increase the chances for successful curriculum adaptations.

8. Assist general educators in anticipating and accounting for potential problems related to the adaptations prior to implementing them.

9. Provide supplemental educational materials to general educators when necessary.

10. Recommend to the general educator, when appropriate, curriculum adaptations similar to those implemented in the special education classroom to ensure consistency in the student's education.

The major area of emphasis for special educators is to provide *support* to general educators in the inclusive classroom. This includes assisting in development or gathering of materials, management ideas, and in general, implementation of curriculum adaptations. Clearly, both special and general educators have important roles in this process. Collaborative efforts that adhere to the guidelines just outlined help to ensure effective adaptations.

Evaluation Stage

It is critically important to evaluate the curriculum adaptation plan. (An evaluation method is presented in the guide in Figure 4.2.) Teachers should monitor the effects of the adaptations by discussing them with students on a daily basis. A simple self-monitoring checklist could be developed and completed by the student each time he or she employs the desired skill related to the objective. When the plan suggests techniques that involve readily observable behaviors, the teacher might also complete a simple daily checklist that indicates the frequency of the observed behaviors. Ongoing monitoring of the program by special and general educators must occur, along with a summative evaluation of the effects upon the desired goal (e.g., improved weekly test scores, increased attention during writing class, number of completed assignments).

In addition to evaluating the effects of specific curriculum adaptations, teachers should also evaluate overall program implementation. This may be accomplished through periodic discussions about the program to identify and resolve problems that may arise. Although minor program changes may be necessary, major changes should be avoided until the program has been completed. Careful and cooperative collaboration during the development stage helps to reduce the need for making major program changes later on. Upon completion of the program, all involved teachers should determine the effects of the adaptations on the desired objective, evaluate the method for implementing the program, and decide upon a subsequent course of action. An understanding among educators of selected issues related to program collaboration assists in the smooth and successful implementation of adaptations in inclusive settings.

Although several important features of this model have been outlined and discussed, the interaction between general and special educators must also be addressed. Well-formulated plans will not succeed if these individuals are not sensitive to each other's needs. Interpersonal relationship skills are crucial to the development, implementation, and evaluation stages of a curriculum adaptation program, and, to a great extent, relate directly to its success or failure. In essence, how educators interact with each other is equally as important as the content of information shared during the curriculum adaptation process.

Collaborative Skills for Effective Adaptations

One of the greatest challenges with which special and general education teachers are confronted is that of working effectively with other educators to ensure appropriate programming in the inclusive classroom setting.

Facilitating the Process of Change

In many situations, the introduction of curriculum adaptations in inclusive settings requires that teachers change one or more aspects within the classroom situation, such as seating arrangements, assignments, teaching strategies, groupings, reward structures, or classroom rules. In addition to teacher concerns, success or failure of the adaptations in inclusive classes rests upon how well the teacher deals with change and how well the special educator assists the teacher in the inclusive classroom in implementing necessary changes resulting from a curriculum adaptation program. Knowledge of the general process associated with creating and implementing change, along with major qualities of curricular change, can help in making curriculum adaptations successful. Miller and Seller (1985) discussed several qualities inherent in change related to curricula implementation and subsequent adaptations. They include recognizing that:

1. Change happens to individuals and is a process rather than a single event.

2. Change involves learning a new skill or developing new meanings, appreciations, or views of existing skills or knowledge.

3. Educators in different roles perceive the meaning of change in different ways.

4. The actual implementation of change is influenced by many events, some of which are not completely in the control of the teacher.

5. Change and its implementation can be facilitated effectively.

6. One ultimate goal is to assist teachers in developing a capacity to change so future changes become easier.

As collaboration among educators occurs, consideration of these qualities facilitates better understanding of different aspects associated with the process. In addition to understanding these qualities, teachers working collaboratively must also be familiar with the general process of change. This process includes several steps or components that apply to change associated with different aspects of a curriculum and the learning environment:

1. awareness of the change possibility;

2. interest in change;

3. time to consider the potential worth of the proposed change; and

4. execution of the proposed change on a small, specific scale prior to full implementation.

Before change occurs, educators must see the need for and the feasibility of implementing it relative to the curriculum adaptations in their classrooms. Once these needs are determined, teachers must be interested in creating change. Obviously, low interest and commitment levels will probably mean low involvement, which often results in little or no change. If necessary, interest in change must be created, and educators may need assistance in seeing its value. Once interest is achieved, educators should outline a program that specifies elements to be included in the implementation of curriculum adaptations, such as the elements discussed previously in the *Guide for Program Implementation of Curricular Adaptations* (see Figure 4.2).

Once the plan has been developed and specific changes outlined, teachers must be given time to consider the value of the proposed adaptation changes. If teachers do not see their value, these changes will probably not occur. The final step in the change process is to allow teachers to implement the adaptations systematically on a small scale and to determine and account for potential problems prior to full implementation. As teachers successfully negotiate these important steps, full implementation of the proposed adaptations occurs.

Although these steps may appear obvious, the chances for success of the proposed curriculum adaptations and associated change improve greatly if the teacher is able to deal with each step. The amount of time required to progress through the steps varies, however. The model for program collaboration (see Figure 4.1) necessitates that this change process be addressed initially in the development stage and emphasized continually throughout the implementation and evaluation stages.

Other elements associated with effective change have also been documented. Additional factors associated with creating and implementing successful change are summarized in Table 4.1. The information in this table applies specifically to program collaboration between special and general educators in the inclusive classroom during the curriculum adaptation process. If change in the implementation process is required, adherence to these principles, along with the information discussed previously, may assist in the successful planning and implementing of curriculum adaptations. Each of the critical factors outlined in the table contributes to effective change. The predominant theme is cooperative planning within a problem-solving structure. Special and general educators should consider these factors as they undertake collaborative efforts related to the development, implementation, and evaluation of curriculum adaptation programs.

Table 4.1

Critical Factors Associated with Effective Change

Success levels associated with change improve as the:

1. Teachers conducting the change work on problems they perceive as important to address;
2. Direction for change is determined cooperatively by the general and special education teachers;
3. Teachers acquire experience related to the issues or tasks that they are changing;
4. Number of factors associated with the change is kept to a minimum;
5. Channels of communication between educators are kept open and honest;
6. Planning for change is completed jointly by those involved;
7. Problem-solving sessions are kept task-oriented and specific to issues necessary to create the change;
8. Special and general educators respect each other's capacities for change (i.e., some people change more rapidly or more slowly than others).

Note. From *Cognitive Learning Strategies for Minority Handicapped Students* (p. 69), by C. Collier and J. J. Hoover, 1987, Boulder, CO: Hamilton Publications. Copyright 1987 by Hamilton Publications. Reprinted with permission.

Requisite Communication Skills

The steps and processes associated with change and curriculum adaptation through program collaboration require use of various communication skills to assist in building and maintaining functional working relationships. Harris and Schutz (1986) and Stewart (1986) identified several abilities and qualities crucial to successful communication and interpersonal relationships in program collaboration. They include

1. knowing our own needs and limits of ability;

2. clarifying our own expectations;

3. conveying respect, empathy, and understanding toward others;

4. establishing and maintaining rapport;

5. becoming effective and careful listeners;

6. avoiding the implementation of solutions until all or most pertinent information has been gathered;

7. supporting other teachers' efforts and needs;

8. being nonjudgmental and tolerant toward others;

9. becoming informed and knowledgeable about the specific issues related to the program collaboration; and

10. introducing knowledge and skills to other educators gradually and systematically in an objective and nonthreatening manner.

Discussion Issues

1. Discuss the guidelines that general and special educators should follow as curriculum adaptations are developed and implemented.

2. Develop and describe a hypothetical or real situation for assisting a teacher in dealing with the steps associated with the process of change.

3. Develop and explain a process for adapting each of the four curricular elements.

4. Discuss how program collaboration related to curriculum adaptations can be facilitated with educators who are reluctant to implement adaptations in their classrooms.

Related Concerns 5

The current practice of inclusion has presented a variety of challenges to general and special educators in their efforts to meet individual learning and behavior needs. In addition, because many students with learning or behavior problems are educated in inclusive settings, efforts to provide appropriate education must include consideration of those students' needs and abilities, as well as consideration of setting variables. This chapter provides information that will help in identifying teacher, parent, and student concerns about specific inclusive situations. Several checklists are presented that will help teachers to better understand each unique situation and the associated student needs. The issues discussed in this chapter address some of the more practical concerns of those involved with educating students who have learning or behavior problems in inclusive settings.

Placement Concerns

Among the many concerns of classroom teachers are issues related to their own perceived abilities to address specific needs in their classes. Student self-assessment related to inclusion provides educators with a beginning point from which the educational program for the student may be implemented effectively. Concerns that relate to the inclusion program of any student must be identified initially to ensure the most successful program implementation. In addition, self-assessment on inclusion issues allows teachers to identify areas in which they (a) may require specific assistance, or (b) must pay particular attention in order to provide an unbiased and appropriate education. Also, to effectively meet individual needs, general and special educators should be aware of each other's concerns related to a specific inclusion situation. The following discussion focuses on helping general and special educators identify their concerns related to the inclusive educational program of a student, along with documenting parent and student concerns. The following guides were derived in part from information found in Gearheart et al. (1996) and Lewis and Doorlag (1995).

General Educator Concerns

A guide to assist in identifying general educator concerns related to the inclusive class placement of a specific student is given in Figure 5.1. This guide reflects some of the major concerns regarding inclusion that may confront the general educator. The items identified in the figure reflect classroom-specific issues, including (a) knowledge of a variety of teaching strategies; (b) skills in the process associated with adapting curricula; (c) testing, grading, and other administrative demands; (d) administrative and special education support; and (e) classroom management issues.

To complete the guide, the general education teacher should place a check next to each item about which she or he has a concern. Although levels of concern will vary from educator to educator, any item for which a potential problem is perceived as a direct result of the inclusion situation should be checked. Space is provided to document other concerns not included, should they be present. The guide should be completed near the beginning of a new inclusive situation for a student and should be redone at regular intervals to ensure that potential problems have been eliminated and that new problems will be identified as early as possible. The guide is designed to be completed for each student in an inclusive situation and should be filled out relative to each content area (e.g., spelling, math, social studies, reading) affected by the placement. If more than one content area is affected, it is important to identify concerns pertaining to each, because these concerns may vary.

Completing the guide should stimulate thought and ideas as to how the identified concerns may be minimized. The first step to ensuring an effective inclusive situation is to identify areas that may or may not present problems. Once identified, they may be directly addressed through a variety of means (e.g., collaboration with special educators, further study related to a specific topic, the use of more efficient organizational or time management abilities). The topics addressed in this book emphasize meeting individual curriculum adaptation needs through collaboration among educators, appropriate adap-

Educator:_____   Student:_____   Subject:_____
Check each item of concern to you as it relates to the mainstreaming of the student in the subject area.

❏ Lack of sufficient training to address student's problem areas
❏ Changes that must be made in the classroom to accommodate student needs
❏ Extra time required for planning
❏ Providing special privileges to the student that others may not receive
❏ Potential disruptions the student may cause during group work times
❏ Potential disruptions the student may cause during independent work times
❏ Interactions with the student's parents
❏ Abilities to adapt curriculum content to meet special needs
❏ Support from the principal and administrators
❏ Support received from special education
❏ Accountability for the student's progress
❏ Dealing with other students' reactions and treatment toward the mainstreamed learner
❏ Identifying specific needs and abilities that must be addressed in the classroom
❏ Extra paperwork required
❏ Sufficient materials to educate the student
❏ Sufficient knowledge of a variety of teaching and behavior management techniques
❏ Testing, grading, and promotion procedures for the student
❏ Interruptions that occur due to the student moving in and out of the classroom
❏ Student's feelings toward own abilities
❏ Student's feelings toward being mainstreamed
❏ Other:

Figure 5.1.   Inclusion concerns form—General educator.

tation of various curricular elements, effective selection and use of a variety of teaching and behavior management techniques, and the effective student use of learning strategies. Each of the concerns identified in Figure 5.1 may be minimized or eliminated through the appropriate use of teaching, study, learning strategies, and effective program collaboration. Completion of this guide by general educators is the beginning of the process of meeting individual needs in the inclusive classroom.

Special Educator Concerns

Special and general educators often share similar concerns related to meeting individual student needs, especially when education is provided in both general and special education classrooms. Several potential concerns of special educators relative to the education of students with learning and behavior problems who are being taught in both special and general education settings are given in Figure 5.2, which is also derived from information in Gearheart et al. (1996) and Lewis and Doorlag (1995).

The items in this figure include (a) potential problems the student may encounter in the inclusive classroom; (b) time for working and collaborating with general educators; (c) sufficient time and materials available to provide an appropriate education; (d) amount and type of work required in both general and special education settings; and (e) administrative and district requirements concerning discipline, management, and curriculum. Space is also provided to include other issues as may be appropriate for particular students.

The procedures for completing this guide are similar to those for Figure 5.1. The special education teacher should check each item that presents a problem relative to a specific inclusive situation. The overall purpose is to give special educators the opportunity to identify concerns that will help them identify (a) areas in which they must improve their skills, or (b) areas of which they must be particularly aware to ensure an unbiased and appropriate education.

The items in the special educator's checklist can be addressed effectively through program collaboration and appropriate selection of teaching, study, and learning strategies presented throughout this book.

The overall process of collaboration as previously discussed may begin by having the special and general educators discuss their concerns relative to meeting individual needs for students with learning or behavior problems.

Family Concerns

In addition to completing guides reflecting concerns of the teachers, both kinds of educators should also complete checklists reflecting their perceptions of parental and student concerns regarding the inclusive situation. Identifying student and/or parent concerns will provide additional information that will be invaluable in understanding the situation.